Michael William Hulse,
Paris, 25 April 1996.

John Tranter grew up on a farm on the south-east coast of Australia. He attended country schools, and dropped out of university after two years' study. With his wife-to-be Lyn, he travelled from London across Europe and Asia in 1967, exploring the hitch-hikers' trail through Turkey, Iran, Afghanistan and India. After working as a cleaner, mail-boy and printer, he returned to university and took his BA in 1970. Since then he has worked mainly in teaching, publishing (including two years in Singapore), and radio production for the ABC, where he was in charge of Radio Helicon in 1987 and 1988. He undertook three reading tours of the USA, England and Europe in the late 1980s. He now lives in Sydney.

He has published widely in Australian, British and American magazines. 'Rain' was published in a recent issue of the *Paris Review*, and a selection of his work appears in the *Norton Anthology of Modern Poetry* (New York, second edition, 1988).

He recently edited (with Philip Mead) the new *Penguin Book of Modern Australian Poetry*, and he is currently the poetry editor of the Sydney-based business/arts weekly the *Bulletin*.

The Floor of HEAVEN

JOHN TRANTER

Angus&Robertson
An imprint of HarperCollins*Publishers*

Arts for Australians Australia Council

CollinsAngus&Roberston Publishers creative writing programme is assisted by the Australia Council, the federal government's arts advisory and support organisation.

AN ANGUS & ROBERTSON BOOK
An imprint of HarperCollinsPublishers

First published in Australia in 1992 by
CollinsAngus&Robertson Publishers Pty Limited (ACN 009 913 517)
A division of HarperCollinsPublishers (Australia) Pty Limited
25-31 Ryde Road, Pymble, NSW, 2073, Australia

HarperCollinsPublishers (New Zealand) Limited
31 View Road, Glenfield, Auckland, 10, New Zealand

HarperCollinsPublishers Limited
77-85 Fulham Palace Road, London W6 8JB, United Kingdom

National Library of Australia
Cataloguing-in-Publication data:
Tranter, John Ernest, 1943-

The floor of heaven
ISBN 0 207 17699X
I. Title.
A821.3

Cover illustration by Tom Woodman (c. 1930)
Typeset in Bembo by Midland Typesetters, Maryborough, Victoria
Printed by Griffin Paperbacks

5 4 3 2 1
96 95 94 93 92

ACKNOWLEDGMENTS

Thanks are due to the editors of the following publications for printing these pieces, often in an earlier draft form: 'Breathless'—to the Melbourne *Age Monthly Review*; 'Gloria'—the Melbourne *Age Monthly Review* published 'Gloria' in an earlier form half its present length, and Nicholas Pounder published that version as a booklet; 'Rain'—to the *Paris Review*; 'Stella'—to *Meanjin* magazine.

I would also like to thank my wife Lyn, who as always offered critical encouragement and support; also Joanne Burns, Jenny Lee, Paul Carter, Martin Duwell, August Kleinzahler and Philip Mead. I would also like to thank Professor W.J.T. Mitchell of the University of Chicago; a conversation we had led to a more ekphrastic focus for 'Stella'.

I would like to thank the Literature Board of the Australia Council for its practical support in various forms over many years, support which has been vital in allowing me to develop my writing. I would also like to thank the Australian Artists Creative Fellowship Advisory panel of the Australia Council for the offer of a recent fellowship, which assisted materially in the completion of these pieces.

—J.T., SYDNEY, 1992.

To my son Leon

How sweet the moonlight sleeps upon this bank!
Here we will sit, and let the sounds of music
Creep in our ears: soft stillness and the night
Become the touches of sweet harmony.
Sit, Jessica: look, how the floor of heaven
Is thick inlaid with patines of bright gold:
There's not the smallest orb which thou behold'st
But in his motion like an angel sings,
Still quiring to the young-eyed cherubins . . .

—*Shakespeare,* The Merchant of Venice

CONTENTS

GLORIA

GLORIA

Gloria handed the doctor a bundle of notes—
typewritten, grubby, scribbled over
and rewritten in different coloured inks.
Masterson adjusted his spectacles
and leafed through the first few pages,
then burrowed further into the mess.
'Yesss, this is interesting, Gloria,
but it looks complicated, full of bother.
Tell me, what does it represent? Hmmm?'
It represented horror, but we didn't
know that then. We dozed, we lazed.
How many of us were there, reclining
peacefully on the grass, sitting in
on the death of the ego. Four? Five? 'Oh,'
Gloria squirmed. 'Oh, it's my . . . well,
memories, where I tell about myself. Talk—
the things . . . you know, where I've been,
what I've done, all that.' Half a dozen of us,
sitting in the pale sunlight in the park
with our sandwiches and bottles of beer: six,
including the troop leader, Doctor Masterson,
who guided the group on its wanderings.
Gloria—twenties, dark hair, freckles
and large round glasses that gave her
the look of a watchful schoolgirl,
wearing a sweet heady perfume that a
teenager might have used—Gloria
frowned and looked down at her hands.

They were twisting slowly in her lap
like dazed, angry creatures. We all
glanced at them, then looked away.
Masterson held a page up to the light
as though something semi-transparent
were hidden underneath the layers of erasures
and white-out, behind the second thoughts
and reconsiderations, a drift, an argument
that might unravel and explain itself
if he stared through it thoughtfully enough.
He puffed on an old pipe, the grey-blue smoke
almost invisible in the hazy light,
though its odour of smouldering heather
drifted over us like a nostalgic memory
and I noticed how the pipe went with his jacket—
dark green tweed, with elbow patches—
to make up a uniform, suited to a character
from an old British movie—a murder mystery
set in some sleepy village before the war—
a doctor, a serious reader, a teacher, perhaps—
and that this message was a kind of pleading:
see me as an uncle, a tutor, a friend,
but not as the fraud I fear I am.

'I think I see what you want.
You'd like one of us to read it out,
is that your plan, Gloria?' He turned
and swung his smile on her like a spotlight.
Was she going to faint? She wavered;
weed under running water. 'Unhhh . . .'
was all Gloria could manage, blushing.
One of the pale animals in her lap

seemed to be on the verge of triumph,
grasping and choking the other, which had
reddened under the sudden attack. A ring—
I hadn't noticed the glittering engagement ring
before—was being twisted violently.

'Well,' she began, 'well, you see . . .
I really can't bring myself to speak . . .
to come out with all that . . . all those . . .
extraordinary . . . events! My goodness!
When I think back over . . . I hoped that
getting it all down in black and white,
turning what happened into a kind of story,
that is, if I could hold back a little way
from all that . . . those terrible memories,
and the good ones, also, because you know
when things are good—so good—they can be
just like a form of torture, too . . . why,
maybe then, with all the blind alleys,
the promises that led to nothing, dreams
that turned into nightmares when you woke—
maybe, crossed out and botched as they are,
it would all fit together, and make sense.'

I noticed her hands were trembling slightly.
She'd been polishing her glasses on the hem
of her print frock, and as she quickly
put them on, she fumbled, and they slipped.
I saw her upper lip was damp with sweat.
She picked the glasses up and pushed them back
on the bridge of her nose with her middle finger.
The gesture was somehow vulnerable, I thought,

or had I read that in a book somewhere—
or seen it in a movie, long ago,
a trick of Bergman's, or Superman's—
she threw a flushed, pleading look quickly
around the group—'And why . . . then you could
perhaps explain it all back to me. Then
I'd know what made it all come out like that,
how—when I was young and full of promise,
so much talent at living—why things all
went so wrong, through no fault of my own,
and everything turned into the most Godawful
mess, and then—' Her voice caught here,
and she struggled to speak—'But I can't—
somehow I couldn't bring myself to spew
forth with all that, in front of everyone,
I just couldn't do that! Do you see?'

She flung a tearful look around the circle
of embarrassed faces like a lasso, but
to no effect. I picked at the grass,
and tried not to look at the others.
I felt sorry for the girl—she seemed
weak, lost, in need of help, and yet
there was something about her voice, her mood—
a clench of hurt, a current of bitterness—
that made me feel anxious and afraid.
I felt sure the story she had to tell—
perhaps not the one she'd given us now,
but some other buried tale too awful
to bring into the light in front of others—
was one that would excite revulsion and fear.

Somewhere in a far recess of summer
monks were playing soccer. The thock
of leather on leather, and their happy cries.

Doctor Masterson's gaze followed her look
at a leisurely pace. He was obviously
searching for someone to saddle with the task
of helping to deliver Gloria's burden
of woe to the world. Looking for a producer,
as it were; a person with tact, someone
who would wade down that black tunnel
that formed Gloria's view of the universe
and bring back treasure, polished, gleaming,
sorted into heaps and counted up;
someone without a stammer or a lisp.
Did we fidget? You bet.

'Oh,
for God's sake,' Gloria said quickly,
and took a deep breath. She held it,
turned pink, and let it out explosively.
Then she gave a short mad laugh. The sun
slipped behind a cloud no one had noticed.

'I had a dream,' she began, then paused.
Her voice had taken on a hard edge
and a querulous tone, as though she had to
win some argument against herself.
'What I wrote, and gave you, that was
the track it followed—not my real career,
but an imaginary one. But in that story,
like a pearl within a pearl shell,

lies another dream—perfect, shimmering.
It's the mirror of another life.

'I had a sister. Her name's Karen. She's—
she's not like me, or my twin Marjorie.
We were poor, and grew up in the country,
and our mother always taught us girls
to hold a straight opinion of ourselves,
never to waver, or sell ourselves cheap,
maybe not to win, but to endure.
But Karen, from the start, was hot-blooded,
younger than us, smaller than me or Marjorie—
and when our mother brought Karen home
from the hospital, it was strange, like
she'd found her there—I don't remember
my mother being pregnant, or any talk
of a little sister—that was a joke
we teased her with, that she was picked up
at a bargain sale in town, dirt cheap,
and Marjorie—she started it—we called her
the lost dog, Karen the Mutt, the mongrel.
We were hoping for a pup, to tell the truth—
I'd been promised an Alsatian for my birthday—
and a kid sister was a disappointment.
She was more a foundling than a relative.
Well, maybe the teasing put an anger in her
that she wouldn't have developed otherwise,
then, maybe she was just bad, the blood
tainted, and nothing you could do about it.
Talk about trouble—you wouldn't believe
the things our family came to later on—
divorce, Marjorie dying, Uncle Ben

ruined, all a result of that girl
and the things she caused to happen.
She looked Nordic, like Mum and Dad,
with pale blonde hair and eyebrows,
and bleached white fuzz on her forearms.
We called her "the Nazi" once—Dad
overheard, and gave us a proper belting.
Grandfather's name had been Larsen,
he changed it to make it more Australian—
the family was Norwegian, or something
Scandinavian, and Mum's mother
came from the Shetlands, a Williams,
like William the Conqueror, a Norman,
descended from the Old Norse raiders.
But Marjorie and I were dark, Celtish,
with black, curly hair and grey eyes—
Dad called us his pair of kelpies.
Karen had these bright blue eyes
the colour of cornflowers, that looked at you
and went right through you like a drill
and out the other side.
'Anyhow—
water long gone under the bridge—
in this dream I'm Marjorie, not myself,
I'm standing to the side, somehow,
just accepting everything that happens;
the dream's about Karen, and she's a real
fuckin bitch.' She took a few quick
deep breaths here, and we all did.
She stood up unsteadily, and paced about,
rubbing her temples, concentrating.
The distant traffic was hushed for a moment.

Two magpies quarrelled in a tree.
Gloria seemed a different woman, taller,
with stronger hands and the flexible body
of a dancer, or an athlete. Somehow her
transformation had won her the gift of fluency.

'Just a moment, Gloria—' said the doctor,
watchful as ever, and careful of his charge,
but his moment had come and gone. 'I'm
Marjorie, right?' said the girl angrily,
'and Karen's talking to me, and I'm listening,
so I can remember everything she says.

' "You know Kellyville?" she says. Marjorie
used to live around that neighbourhood.
"I know Kellyville," I say. "Out past
Blackacre way, boy, what a shithole!"
My voice is booming around, a kind of echo—
I can see myself like a reflection.
"Right on," Karen agrees. "I was there—oh,
ten years back, with that animal I married.
Now why would I marry a creep like that? Me,
my father's pet, the original Princess!
Why would I do a fuckin stupid thing
like that? Can you tell me, Marjorie?"

'I didn't know why she married
a turkey like that,' says Gloria, 'but it's
typical of Karen to pick some loser—
most of her boyfriends were junkies. But
it's just a story that blooms within a dream
like a crystal of some mineral salt

growing at the bottom of a forest pool,
and those things don't have a past, that's
the great gift they have for us, their value,
they come unmarked by childhood guilt, they
drag no chain of nightmares in their wake,
they spring from a limbo of innocence.
But people,' she says, and gives that
mad laugh again—'real people
do self-destructive things, don't they,
they bruise and damage those around them
because they've dragged their fears
behind them like a pack of mad dogs,
to the point where they can do fuckall else.
Am I right? Yes! They make their own
lack of choice by the choices they make,
and they just have to swallow it,
shit or champagne, like it or not.

'But Karen wouldn't be interested in
that kind of philosophical talk.
She was busy with the story of her life
like it was a movie, or a soap opera.
Marjorie patiently listening, that's me.

'"Poor bloody Blake," Karen says.
"I met him one night—I was dropping pills,
floating and stumbling around in my usual daze
when there he was—a big handsome brute.
He worked hard, drank with his mates,
had a hot car, a Thunderbird
painted red like a fire engine.
And a wonderful place at the Cross,

high up in the heavens, with a rooftop
where we drank whisky and champagne
and looked at the stars in the sky, and the clouds
lit with a pale pink-orange colour
from the lights you could see twinkling
down below. That's what I love
about Sydney—it's never dark, never
like that inky dark you get in the bush
when it's cloudy—here the night sky
is always lit up with a warm glow
from people working, driving about, eating,
making love with the lights on, being alive.
Blake was fun to be with, laughed a lot
when we went out, or when his mates
dropped around with a carton or two of beer;
but then he had another side to him—
Mum would say 'Street angel, home devil'.
When he was at home, he had his moods,
like some captive brooding in a cage.

'"Then that recession came along,
there were a lot of people out of work,
and Blake—he had a fight with his boss,
a big Samoan fellow, and got the sack.
Next thing we're both on the dole,
and then he had to let the car go.
Then we had to get a cheaper flat.
And he starts reading books and magazines.
Going to the library, borrowing books,
reading into the night. I have to
get my sleep, or I get awful . . .
difficult to live with. You know?"

"Oh, I know," I say. "It's like that
with me, with drink. Or it used to be."'

Could it be, I asked myself, our shy
Gloria, the freckles, the cheap frock,
a drunk? No—it's possible, but
hard to believe—but then it's this
Marjorie creature who's speaking, some
alter ego perhaps, the two faces of Eve,
or more . . . under the skirts of rectitude
the nymphomaniac, behind the proper
bank president howls the alcoholic.

'Carry on, sweetheart, get it out,'
says Gloria—Marjorie—' "Well," says Karen,
"Blake's father—he'd been dead for years,
but Blake had been through a bad time
with him, long ago. I knew that Bruce,
the brother, the same age as Blake,
volunteered for service in Vietnam
and never came back, and the father
blamed Blake somehow, for being idle,
for not going too. Bruce was tough,
a heart like an ox, full of courage,
and did things proper, by the book;
Blake was lazy, happy-go-lucky,
good-natured. But the father argued,
picked on Blake a lot, and one day
they had a bad fight—what happened,
the details, he wouldn't say at first.
He didn't want to talk about his past.
Till one night, when it came out—

' "It began with the books. He'd bring them home.
And drink this cheap wine, from a flagon,
and sit up late, reading, mumbling
while he followed the words with his finger,
a chuckle, a murmur, rising and falling.
It got on my nerves. Then late at night,
stinking of that cheap after-shave
he wore, he'd want to read them to me, these
magazines, anthologies. 'C'mon, honey,'
he'd say, 'this is a really great story,
about this elephant hunter, an adventure,
just let me read you some of it.' Jesus!

' "It started out a kind of bed-time game,
like, at first, the stories, they were kind of
sexy—not from cheap tit magazines, no—
books, classy magazines with nice photos,
the models young, with tasteful makeup,
real authors and all that, but kind of . . .
well, you know. Then, later on,
they grew more intellectual—Blake,
he'd done a course, some university degree
by mail, he'd worked on an oil rig
back in the sixties, all that free time,
so he did this diploma and learnt to read
intellectual books. Then, to make it crazier,
soon it was no sex without a story.
That's what he said. Can you believe that?
He wouldn't, or he couldn't do it any other
way, without this stupid fuckin twist.

' "And soon it was just this one story,

time after time, about a blind man,
how his wife's lover—a soldier, captured
in Korea and brainwashed, and turned loose
to assassinate the top men in government—
got his wires crossed and murdered ordinary
men and women—a butterfly collector,
an old rabbi, a man selling toys
on the street—well, this crazy pair
plotted to murder her blind husband,
creeping through the house, playing jokes—
that's sick, isn't it? Don't you think?"

'Karen had this ring on her finger,'
Marjorie—Gloria—said, looking at her own
engagement ring, 'and being Karen it was
some cheap rhinestone article
she'd picked up at the Cross, and she
rubbed it and stared at it, and laughed.

' "Enough is enough," she says, in a flat voice,
"what with the drinking and the crying—
did I tell you that? He'd get upset
when he reached the final episode
where the blind man stabs the soldier—
he'd made a special white cane, sharpened
at the end, and he pokes his eyes out
and blinds him, so they're both stumbling around
covered in blood, stabbing at the air—
and Blake's voice would give out here,
he'd start trembling, staring at the page,
wiping his face. It was like a madhouse,
me in bed in my nightdress—a pretty thing,

a pastel blue silk effect, I bought it
in L.A., on that trip to Disneyland,
remember?—perfume, make-up and all,
Blake drunk and wailing like a loon.
Well, Christ, it had to stop. I said
I was packing up and leaving—then
he told me about his father, how they fought,
and how Blake stabbed him in the face—
Oh God, this is horrible! Horrible!"

'And Karen burst into tears,' says Marjorie—
Gloria—and she starts sobbing too, *her* face
swollen and red. Grief, like a layer-cake!

Doctor Masterson poked at his neglected pipe,
and cleared his throat several times.
He was obviously moved by this complex tale
of wretchedness and desperation. He
grimaced and took some tablets from a pocket—
'Indigestion, please excuse me,' and to Gloria:
'My dear girl—your imagination,
you must use more discipline, more
artistic control—and please sit down,
you make me nervous, stalking around behind me
like that—' he dug some tissues
from his jacket—Gloria's handkerchief
was wet with tears—but in the brief moment
it had taken us all to gather our wits,
she had gathered hers. 'I'm Marjorie, okay?'
she spat out, and plunged onward—
'and Karen's explaining to me about
the fight that mutilated Blake's father:

' "They drank heavily, the whole family—
Blake was an alcoholic," Karen said;
"and the mother was into the cooking sherry.
You remember Auntie Eleanor, Marjorie?
'Just a refresher, for the cook!' she'd say,
folding her apron and picking up
a tray of scones, or whipping up a batter,
but sipping at the sherry in between—
remember? Uncle Ben telling blue jokes
and stuffing cakes into his face—God,
that man could eat like a horse—
and mixing his home brew, everybody
laughing in the kitchen, Old Jack
calling by with a brace of wild ducks—
'Hullo, Missus—I just saw these two
sittin' on the dam, and I reckoned
you could use 'em for dinner, so I
nipped back to the shed and got me gun!'
God, Marjorie, the times that are gone . . .
well, like I was saying, Auntie Eleanor,
Blake's mum was like her, but worse.

' "One night—it must have been a Sunday,
and they'd come home early from the Club,
they'd lit the fire in the sitting room,
and turned on a lamp, but the dining room
was dim and shadowy, the mantel clock ticking—
don't they give you the creeps?—the radiogram
playing some dance tune from the thirties
in another room—So there was Jock,
Blake's father, thin as a weasel,
not like the boys; drunk, hacking away

at the roast lamb—he'd wolfed down
his dinner, and he wanted second helpings—
splashing gravy on the good linen tablecloth
they kept for Sunday best, the mother crying,
and Jock going on about the blacks, how they
soak up the government handouts, never work,
drink Blue Ruin, and all that racist shit,
and how Blake's brother was a real man,
never shirked his duty, lion-hearted,
Bruce knew what he wanted, volunteered
for service, killed a few Vietnamese,
and he'd put the Abos in their place.
Blake was keen on a young girl at the time,
part Aborigine, bright, and very pretty.
He swallows as much as he can take, then
he gives a scream like a stuck pig
and a red mist floods over his eyes
and then—it goes blank, no sound,
all dark, he can't remember a thing.

' "Just as well, for what he did then—
the carving knife—Blake had a fetish
about sharpening things, he had
a grindstone, and an Arkansas stone,
and a steel like butchers use, he'd go
whip, *whip*, like that, honing the edge
till it sparkled like a scalpel blade—
in this fit of rage he grabbed the knife
and he cut his father's face about so horribly
that the old man lost both his eyes,
chopped up like soft-boiled eggs. And
the carving fork, with those long prongs,

he drove it right up through his father's nose
with one blow, the thin sinus bones,
right through the floor of the brain cavity,
was how Blake described it. Cut the brain,
a fraction, just a snip, a pointed cut,
right through where your memories are joined,
where you remember things, and store them away.
The ambulance man had to pluck it out,
the long fork, stuck deep in the skull,
and bits of flesh all over the tablecloth.

'"Well, Jock lived—a bit of surgery,
no problem, but his eyes were gone, and worse,
his brain was damaged so that he never
remembered any new thing again.
His early memories lingered on: school,
who he was, old train timetables,
the scent of a pine tree cut down,
a movie he'd seen years ago and could
tell you the plot, telephone numbers,
addresses, bets he'd had on the horses—
but nothing he ever learnt from that day on
stuck. Well, you can imagine Blake, the blame,
the guilt! Whatever he could do to make it up,
he tried, because he really loved his dad.
And then the Aboriginal girl left,
shot through with the father of her baby,
some creep from Tokyo, a priest. The mother
seemed to fade away, Blake said,
hardly eating, pecking like a sparrow,
just a few crumbs here and there,
and in the end she got so thin

she lost her will to live—the bloodshed
had shocked her terribly, and her heart
was weakened by the drink, and diabetes—
so she died, and left them, father and son,
the two of them, together in the house.

' "Like poor Auntie Eleanor, in her last days.
You used to write to me each week—remember?—
when you went to boarding school in the city,
and tell me how you'd go out to visit,
to the old people's home, and read to her
from the family Bible—all that way
alone on the tram, in the evening,
to read the Old Testament, and she'd sob
and hold a dirty hankie to her mouth—
old age, it's a terrible thing. And Gloria,
that bitch, too busy with her books
and her university friends to help out,
too busy drinking gin and having abortions
and being smart and intellectual, and me
stuck on the bloody farm. Oh, I'm sorry,
but those things make me angry. Old Jock.

' "Blake read to him at night—his dad
was blind, and he hated advertisements,
so the TV and the radio were out.
And he refused to listen to the ABC,
full of fuckin communists, he said.
Reading. Every evening. That was fine,"
Karen says, "Blake didn't mind. But you see,

' "every time he'd start to read a story,

poor Jock would forget it by the time
his son had reached the bottom of the page.
'How did that begin again?' he'd say. 'That
sounds like a bloody good yarn. How does it go?'
and Blake would have to start the page again.
There was one story he particularly liked,
from an old *Playboy* magazine, about a guy
who made a living killing elephants.
There was a sex interest in it somewhere,
but Blake never got that far. Over and over,
page thirty-seven, where the story starts
in Nairobi, buying up supplies, then the hero
gets drunk in a bar, and fights a Negro.
Night after night, that page, for seven years.
Then his father had a stroke—he was
getting on, in any case—had a stroke
and sat there in the nursing home, drooling,
eating up money, that's how Blake put it,
and the doctors like a flock of vultures,
till his mind went blank—just nothing—
and he was gone, and Blake was left alone.

' "I picked Blake up," Karen says,
"in a singles bar, soon after that.
I thought: at last, here was a real doll—
he looked stunning in his red convertible—
a big hunk of a guy, built like a house,
a gentle gorilla—someone to sweep me
off my feet and make up for the bad times:
what happened on the farm, Uncle Ben,
working the street, the trouble with the cops.
He wasn't Robert Redford, but he had

a sense of humour, and he took me out a lot.
His eyes were grey, his glossy black hair
fell in thick waves over his collar,
he looked so cute in the clothes he wore,
the roll-neck sweaters, duffel jackets.
He polished up nice, on a lady's arm.
It was fun for a while. He was good in bed,
at first, then he began to get moody, then
the stories started, then the madness.

' "He drank, and in the end he lost his job,
and we were thrown out of our flat, and moved
to that joint way past Kellyville—
we hardly had any money, except for wine—
then to a basement dump in Darlinghurst—
you had to climb down a flight of stairs,
damp sweat on the walls, mould,
dark and freezing in winter, we always
had the light on even in the daytime
and you hardly ever got to see the sky,
and in summer you'd think it would be cool,
but it was suffocating, like a furnace.
And Blake got obsessed about his hair—
he even had nightmares about it—
how it was going grey, and receding,
and then it was falling out, going bald—
I'd catch him with a comb in his hand,
standing in front of the mirror, crying.

' "Then one day, a knock on the door,
and the strangest creature was standing there
weaving from foot to foot in the shadows

like a circus bear—it was Bruce, the brother.
The war was over, and the Vietnamese,
after they'd tortured the poor man
half to death and back, had patched him up
and sent him home again. He looked awful—
big, but bent, hunched over stiffly,
a grey-blond thatch of hair, freckles
that mottled his face like a disfigurement,
and his blue eyes had a crazy glitter.
And there was something wrong with his mouth;
he came up close, and I saw he had a hare-lip
that gave him a strange, sarcastic kind of sneer.
Blake had never told me about that, and then
I realised there were no photos of Bruce—
you'd think when someone close to you
had disappeared off the face of the earth
there'd be a shrine of some sort, but no,
not even a holiday snap, and that was why.
There was a smell about him I didn't like—
beer, tobacco, a kind of animal sweat.
'My brother,' he grunted, 'A souvenir
for my brother.' His big fat paws
held out a parcel wrapped in newspaper—
the back of his hands were matted with red hair—
I felt it, something cold and heavy,
but he wouldn't let me take it, he pushed past
and went through the flat like a robot
calling out 'I want my brother!'
He found Blake half asleep, hungover.
Bruce grabbed him and yelled out loud—
'You fucking mongrel, what did you do?
I want to talk to my dad!'

then he started beating poor Blake
and cracking his head against the wall
for what he'd done on that Sunday
with the knife and the carving fork.
I ran to the kitchen to get something
to hit him with—there was a leg of lamb
I'd just taken from the freezer, I grabbed it
and ran back to the bedroom—he'd taken
a grenade from the parcel, and pulled the pin,
and he was holding Blake against his chest
in a bear-hug, groaning and howling.
I swung the leg of lamb and brought it down
crack on the back of his skull, grabbed Blake—
he'd been beaten nearly unconscious—
and pulled him out of there. We were
halfway down the hall when it went off,
a terrible bang!—and I woke up in hospital.

' "Blake said later that he'd crawled back
to try to help Bruce, or to apologise,
but there were just pieces everywhere.
What he saw stuck in his memory
like some horror movie episode
repeating over and over. From then on
he was never quite the same. His skull
had been fractured by the beating, they said,
and his eardrums blown in by the grenade,
so he was half deaf from then on,
though he could hear his 'special voices',
he told me, chiding him for little things
like stealing and dishonesty, and Blake said
'I'm a murderer, but they never mention that.'

Isn't that sad? I cried when he said that.
The doctors patched him up—his eyesight
was never right, and he had to wear glasses,
and they gave him anxiety pills to take
but they made his hands shake, and when he drank
they mixed badly with the alcohol, and then
he'd knock into things and fall over.
And all the time, remembering the grenade,
trying to forget, to blot it out,
then his father, and the meat knife—
he went to group therapy for a while,
but he used to argue, and yell at the doctor.
I was optimistic—he had a medical pension;
there couldn't be any more family trouble—
there wasn't any family, for a start.
I hoped that he could pull himself together.

'"He got his job back with the Samoan,
but then he started stealing—a stuffed bird,
an emu egg, a butterfly display—
and so they had to give him the sack again.
In the end—no medication seemed to work,
and he was drunk or drugged all the time,
with a dull stare like a pole-axed bullock—
he started seeing things, wanting to die—
in the end they put him away, and every night
I think of him locked in there, growing old,
flinching at the voices criticising him,
the endless torrent of memories, the poor man
desperate for things to be like they were,
to turn the clock back, and start again.

' "Oh, Marjorie, I can't bear it!" Karen says,
and a shiver runs through her thin body.
She takes her glasses off and rubs her eyes
and hides her face in her hands.' And Marjorie
was sniffing, holding back a tear, and
Gloria was obviously wrung out, too,
but she had a strange look in her eyes—
they were wet with tears, but they glittered—
she was happy, that was it, her grey eyes
sparkling! She laughed, and hugged herself,
and held her face up to the sky. Then
she sat down at last, with a shudder.

The sun drifted out from behind a cloud
and a warm light spilled across the park.
We frowned and blinked in the glare, like
strangers wandering out from a midday movie.

'My notes, please, Doctor Masterson,' she said,
and took back those sheets of type and scribble.
I noticed that her hands were shaking slightly.
Masterson stared at her. No one said a thing.

'Let's start at the beginning, then, shall we,
where I have this extraordinary dream.' Gloria
smiled, adjusted her glasses, and began.

STELLA

STELLA

We'd gone—half a dozen of us—from
a gathering at Doctor Masterson's,
headed for The Newcastle, when a shower
swept across the park and drove us
into the doorway of the nearest building.
'It's Florenzini's!' said the Saint—
'Let's go in and wait out the rain.'

The restaurant downstairs was busy
with its usual noisy crowd of students,
artists and hangers-on, but upstairs
the bar was almost empty. A jukebox
played a Miles Davis track from the fifties.
An old friend of Doctor Masterson's
wandered in and joined us—he was known
as the Captain of Industry, a bulky man
with reddish hair and a smouldering cigar.

Max was speaking. He was new to the group,
and still burdened with a half-told
tale he had to tell—there was a sin
he wanted to confess, or perhaps a crime.
We weren't the ideal audience: Professor Flack
glancing idly through the *TLS*,
the Saint restless and European, Sandra
making quiet asides, lighting cigarettes:
one joining another at the window
and murmuring together. From outside,

the sound of buses sweeping through the rain.

'I was stuck in a narrow corner,' Max said,
ravelling a skein of woe he'd been
entangled in earlier that afternoon.
'I was mad about Stella, and I knew
she loved me.
'But differently—women
are women—and for different reasons.
But what was I to do? She'd gone back
to that fool her husband, the "editor"—
dilettante, scribbler, amateur capitalist,
her wonder boy ruined every paper
he touched, a trail of wrecked companies—
yet people called him a genius! He skipped
from one deck to the next as the ship sank—

'Damn it all, she didn't break it off,
she did worse, she made it just possible
but painful to go on with the affair,
small towns are always hives of gossip—
every country town a prison-house—
cut off like that, stranded on the
rocks of loneliness and hostile snooping,
what was I to do?' he asked, sadly.
He poured his drink into his mouth, wiped
his chin, and plunged into reminiscence—

Stella's apron tied back at her waist,
the way she ran a comb through her hair
and laughed like a self-conscious starlet
in a 1940s beach picnic movie, the surf

embroidering the line between
what life gives us—what we get—
and what we can't have, and the summer sun
spilling through the green crests of the waves
as the water folds over and dissolves into foam . . .

'These memories are all she left me,
ashes in the mouth, and those promises,
when we met, we seemed so young—
I'll start at the beginning,' he said—
The beginning? I felt that his love,
or the lack that made up his need for love
must have begun in some distant schoolyard,
in a tightening circle of desertion and
torment, but to begin where he began—

'I lost my lovely wife and made a packet
on the horses in the same week, so
I retired to Hartford, a small town
near the coast, I'd grown up there,
I knew few people—so I settled in
with a pack of cards, a wine cellar,
a library—well, a load of old books
I'd been wanting to read for donkey's years—
Toxophilus, Burton's *Anatomy*, James Jones,
Joyce Cary, Callimachus and Cavafy—

'but things never work out quite
the way you plan.' Sandra reappeared
bright-eyed from the Ladies' Powder Room
just in time to catch the reading list, and
approved cheerfully. 'I've been reading

Portrait of the Artist,' she began—'Wrong
artist, I mean writer,' Max interrupted,
'Pearl Harbour and the Liffey aren't the same—'
'Writer, whatever, you know the Irish,
cunning, often exiled, seldom silent,'
Sandra went on, checking her lipstick
in a mirror. 'They suffer an affliction
hardly their own fault—the self-hatred
of a proud people too often
invaded and humiliated,' and she reached
for her drink, an Advokaat and Cherry Brandy.

'Do go on,' whispered the Saint, to Max;
and to Sandra: 'Dear, you finished it,
and they took the glass away, umbrella and all.'

'I joined the Bridge Club,' Max went on,
'I needed company more than cards, I think,
but then the subtle social need is always
the underlying motive, from gambling
to work, from sex to psychotherapy.
Fishing and photography are
the only truly solitary vocations.
Have you ever tried to chat with
a fisherman? Or shared a darkroom? So.

'I couldn't even play bridge at first—
I was miserable, it rained, cloud
drifted in over the breakwater,
I was brooding too much on things
that had passed away long ago.
The Bentons were very social—dances,

evenings at the Club—it was their need
for drink that drove them, it seemed to me,
though they couldn't bear to drink alone
together. And they played bridge, though
they made a bad pair, with their bitching.

'I partnered Stella the first time
I tried to learn the game, one evening—
a stormy winter night—rain blowing
through the garden, screen doors banging
in the wind—the perfume she wore,
there was something fresh and innocent
about it, a delicacy, but underneath
a smoky, dark colouring—God help me,
I fell in love like that!'
He snapped his fingers.
'Half an hour, that's how long it took.
Stella. Benton's lovely young wife.
Twenty years ago, it must have been.'

'Oh, the forties,' the Saint broke in,
his accent—Hungarian, perhaps—
lending a sarcastic curl to what he said.
'Spivs in flying jackets, dud penicillin
at ten quid a dose, black-market nylons—
a phoney culture, rotten right through,
that laid the ground for beatniks and drugs—
jazz, dark glasses, French philosophy—'

'My shout,' said Doctor Masterson. 'Bruno!'
There was a bustle and a bother, fresh drinks
were poured and passed around. 'I remember

she was drinking Dutch gin that night,'
Max went on. 'You forget so much, and yet
certain images—symbolic, perhaps—
there must be some psychological theory
to explain these things, eh, Professor?'
Flack looked up from the crossword. 'Mmmm?
Theory? Well, the new ones are linguistic.
I'm not sure they've invented one
to handle nostalgia. I could whip one up,
if you like. Let's see—"Reified Desire:
Temporal Recuperation and the Other."
How's that?' With a chuckle he sank back
into the *Times*. Max frowned. Was he being
sent up? He couldn't be sure. He went on.
'The lamp, for example, I hadn't noticed
when I sat down to play, and I'd seen it
perhaps a dozen times before—but now
I noticed, with an inexplicable sharpness,
its exact shape—I could draw it
for you now, twenty years later—
a blackened bronze figure of a girl
holding up a globe that glowed softly . . .'
'Oh, a Gloria lamp,' Masterson mused,
'we used to have a girl once, in the group—'
but Max had ploughed ahead—
'I can see
the peach-tinted light along her arm,
and hear the faint tapping of her nails—
bright scarlet polish—on the card—
would she deal it now, or hold it back?—
a diamond, I think—perhaps a heart—
but it was red, exactly the tint

of her nails and the lipstick she wore . . .
she drained her glass of gin—rain
on the roof, wind thrashing the garden,
so loud you could hardly hear
the chatter and the laughter, the clink
of glasses being filled . . . so long ago . . .'

His voice drifted into silence. For a moment
we all seemed lost in a mist of memories.
Sandra broke the spell. 'Oh,' she shivered,
'An angel just walked over my grave.'

'Love hit us both at the same moment,
or should I say passion, or infatuation—
but we only learned that later,'
Max said, 'so we sat there
playing a weak, erratic, losing game.
Then the stratagems, hesitancies,
a kind of delirium, where not quite knowing
is the most delicious phase, your life balanced
exactly on the knife-edge, a kind of terror,
your heart pumping, the room full of silence,
but such a heavy quiet—unbearable—'

'Ah Christ! The limo!' cried the Captain,
and bolted for the door. 'Well,' the Saint
murmured, 'now where's the Big Chief
off to?'
                'Has to shift his car,
left it outside with the engine
running, his *limousine*,' Sandra said,
giving the word a French inflection.

'You've met him, haven't you?' enquired
Professor Flack, in a low, private tone.
His eyes were a weak, watery blue,
and they fixed me in an analytic stare.
'The Captain's an old friend of Masterson's,
worked in Intelligence together in the War,
in the East, apparently, lost his son
in Korea, missing in action, never found,
don't you think that would be terrible,
never really knowing? I mean, he might be
cranking out propaganda in some dungeon
under the Yalu, chained to a bench . . . The father
threw himself into business, like a shark,
they reckon, never comes up for air,
tossed in the art game, so they say,
never picked up a brush again,
a dealer I know said What a loss
to Australian Art, Incalculable, but
you never know, who can predict,
talent's a dickey thing in my experience,
of course the first wife's another matter.
How's your drink, all right? Hullo,
they're at it again.' I turned to catch Max
arguing with the Saint. 'Rubbish, this
dream of yours,' Max was saying,
'just because a sequence of images
is tangled and bizarre, and laced or
doped with a confused, cloudy mood,
do we have to listen to it all
respectfully? Real life, yes,
recollected in tranquillity, or
rather, passion, there's a guarantee

of relevance. A tale that really happened!
What can be more meaningful than that?'

'Slow down, Max,' Sandra chided, 'Your
motives are showing, and you're growing flushed.'

'What I mean,' the Saint went on
reflectively, brushing his collar, 'is that
under the struggle to drag our lives
above the level of daily dull endurance
an appetite arises for the subterranean,
and so we press against the dark glass doors
of the unconscious, that let us glimpse
what is hidden yet disguise our worst urges—
dreams are our own gestures magnified
in that glass, that countryside—'
he waved at a large landscape painting
hung at one end of the bar, the frame
like a picture-window giving onto a view
of a pale coast, cottages stacked up
along a strip of grey sand, the wind
flecking the sheet of blue with whitecaps—

'Max, continue!' shouted the Captain,
who had returned wet from the rain.
He waved a damp, half-eaten cigar.
I noticed his disarray for the first time—
his tie had come undone and hung loose,
and the suit that had started out as
a symbol of his standing in the City now
spoke of decline—ash littered the cuffs,
a large handkerchief ballooned

from a sleeve, a shirt pocket bled
with a spreading stain of purple ink.
'Max! The knife-edge! The deck of cards!'

'Stella and I,' Max said, 'Yes,
we were soon practising to deceive, ah,
the pattern seems to weave itself a little
differently each time I recall it,
so that now I'm not sure exactly what
happened—when we first made love,
for example, was it raining . . . in my car,
or hers?—her husband's ranch wagon, rather,
an old Nash with fake wood panelling.

'I gave up bridge—we were too obvious,
staring at each other, blushing, losing
one trick after another. But
we had to go on meeting somehow,
and plausibly. Oh,
                                        why did I do it?'
'Do what?' shot Professor Flack.
'Like a fool,' said Max, 'just to be close,
I learned photography as best I could,
and talked her husband into giving me a job
on the paper he managed. To be near Stella,
that was the idea, but it backfired
dreadfully. Oh, I saw Stella,
but it cost a packet, all the tackle
you need, and I made a mess of it,
I broke a new enlarger and I ruined
seven rolls of film in the developer.'

'Oh, photography, you men!'
Sandra put in—she was on her third
Advokaat and Cherry Brandy, and her cheeks
had a warm flush—'If ever an art form
was crippled by its plausibility!
I've spent a lifetime in a darkroom—
the history of the medium's a tug-of-war
to free the image from its corresponding
form in the so-called real world,
but politics—who looks at that?
As vital an ingredient in any
photographic lab as sodium sulphite.
Look at the States in the early 1950s,
Sid Grossman shooting the working class
at play, frightened off the boardwalk
by McCarthy and the middle class,
retreating from Coney Island to Cape Cod!
And Lisette Model, already a refugee.
"The Fifties?" she said, "It was terrible.
You didn't know what to photograph." '

'Well, I shot what I was pointed at,'
Max replied, 'it was a country paper—
cows, Mrs Clampitt's chrysanthemums,
the fish Doctor Rampart caught (but not
the doctor's best catch, his gypsy mistress,
a fortune-teller from a travelling circus),
the dog show, the cat show, pigs . . .

'but the jinx! Every roll of film—
I got the speed wrong, or the flash
short-circuited, or the developer

was exhausted and needed replenishing.
And Stella—I could feel her slipping away,
and each day I loved her more, my heart,
it was horrible, watching her indifference
grow. And the amateur capitalist,

'he knew, he found out about us
somehow, how, I can't imagine—
he sent me further afield, interstate,
once, with impossible assignments—
he sent me to a seance to photograph
the "ectoplasm" or the "emanations"
on infra-red film, of course I took
the wrong film, there are several types,
apparently, a scientific one,
colour, monochrome, and so forth,
and then a game-fishing competition,
it was raining—he was laughing at me,
I can see it now—I had to get
the shark's-eye view, looking up
through the ripples at the idiots
and sea water leaked through the lens,
how was I to know? I ruined it,
a Nikon, an expensive camera,
a present from Stella, when we first met.
He was pushing me too hard,
the bastard, and I snapped, I fought back,
I tackled him one day, and had it out.
Do you know what he said? Can you imagine
what the office-boy scribbler said to me?'

Max's eyes were bulging out of their sockets,

and though their magnetism held the others
in a staring group like a disordered
'Night Watch' redesigned by Grosz,
the Captain seemed immune—his voice murmured
at my ear: 'Something I want to show you',
and I found myself being led down
to the basement. There, Florenzini's
grew more complex than I'd remembered
or imagined—rooms within rooms,
one bar concealed behind another,
doors marked 'Private', 'Club Room',
'Gallery' and 'Staff Only'. The Captain
led me by the elbow through this maze
and down a further flight or two of stairs.
'Ignore this rubbish,' he muttered, his mouth
working from some inner psychic pressure,
his voice cramped by the atmosphere
of the place we'd entered. It was a gallery—
though the pale blue underwater lighting,
the heavy curtains—acres of indigo,
decorated with tiny yellow diamonds
outlined in green—and a huge bowl
of purple gladioli in a corner
gave it the atmosphere of a chapel, or
the Tomb of Mausolus. A faint scent of cigars
hung on the air. How had we got here?
Only a moment ago I'd been with Max
drinking in the upstairs bar, and now
I was the prisoner of a man mumbling unhappily
and dragging me past a large Blackman—
a giggle of schoolgirls in a florist's shop—
a Whiteley fluent with the jargon

of advertising, and a tiny etching
that I felt certain was a Rembrandt.
We paused—he put his arm around my shoulder
and I noticed with a kind of shock
that his hair—dark reddish-brown,
like an orang-utan's—was in fact a wig,
dyed rather crudely, and badly fitting.
His moustache, it now seemed to me,
was dyed too. 'You know art, I believe,'
he said. 'What d'you think of this, eh?'
We'd come to rest at last, in front of a painting.

It was some kind of dream scene—
a large impasto piece, heavily worked,
and layered over with a coat of varnish—
its gestures both Romantic and Expressionist,
though the style was oddly fresh. Figures
collided with bulky slabs of landscape
and struggled with a clutter of symbols.
Clowns wept, harpies cackled, and demons
writhed and gestured from the branches above.
The background was a pool of swirling black
out of which glowed red and yellow stars.

'Worrying, isn't it?' the Captain said,
looking at me with a peculiar smile.
Then he looked at the painting again, and sighed,
and ran his fingers through his absurd hair.
His forehead was sweating, his chin
badly shaved, and I noticed dark circles
of exhaustion under his eyes—he's been crying,
I thought.

'Well, this woman I used to know
painted it. It's clever, lots of thought
went into the figures—social comment,
half of them are artists or philosophers,
half bureaucrats and journalists—
Patrick White said that in Australia
the schoolmaster and the journalist rule
what intellectual roost there is—
there's technique to take your breath away,
and there's passion—well, anger, at least.
But is it the Real Thing? God knows.

'I said it was good. Years ago, now.
I said it was greatly talented,' he went on,
and tossed back his glass of wine. 'I said
it was very brave, in the generosity
of love, but love is blind, they say,
and art's for looking at, not bleating about.
But then I don't really understand art,
despite owning acres of the stuff.

'What are those card players supposed to
represent, eh? That Fat Man,
whom d'you suppose he really is?
The Devil? She had visions, you see,
she'd telephone, always late at night,
the dead hour, she'd wake up the house,
babbling in that broken lingo she spoke:
disasters—a fighter plane shot down,
a crowded ferry capsized and sunk,
an oil rig exploding in a ball of flame—
Paint it, I'd say, trying to whisper,

sketch it out, embroider the bloody thing,
make a painting of it, distance yourself.
And always these figures, the Fat Man,
the Devil, the Lost Child on the edge
of an abyss, flames colouring the sky . . .

'I told her to see a doctor, a psychiatrist,
a priest even, someone to talk to.
Look, my wife's an understanding woman,
but these phone calls at the dead of night,
we'd arrive home from the opera—
Wagner, say, the Valkyries clattering
across the roof of Heaven, and the phone
would be jangling—I presume it's for you,
my wife would say, drily, and sail away
down the hall, and the voice a babble
from the receiver—we had an old black
bakelite telephone, my dad knew Leo Baeke,
the plastics inventor, in New Jersey—
he called himself Baekeland in America—
we kept it for some sentimental reason,
even when the family—Baeke's nephew,
grandson, who was it? killed his mother,
not Baeke's, the boy's mother, murdered,
mad, they said, the boy, the mother too,
and sexually twisted with it, but the words,
they poured out of the heavy black handset
in a stream, what could I say? Paint it
out of you, I'd say, halfway
between a shout and a whisper, let it out,
give the devils a name and a habitation.

'So what are they pointing at? Is there
some kind of symbolism in that?
Estelle, her name was, God help me,
gone these many years.' Six figures,
grotesquely masked, were pointing at a table
in the lower centre of the picture.
It held a carafe of pink wine, a broken
loaf of bread, a dozen playing cards.

'It's more tangled the more I dwell on it,'
he went on. 'She had the baby, but then
she farmed it out, with relatives back home,
I suspect, though she'd never tell
where exactly, in which vermin-ridden,
plague-rotted cluster of muddy huts . . .
"How could I bring it up," she'd say,
"Living like this, my suicidal rages,
a slave to the Demon Alcohol, and a willing one"—
that's how she'd talk, when she was desperate—
"eating crusts" (—I pushed money on her,
I had enough, she threw it back at me),
"and the men" (—there were other men,
what could I do? Love!) "and those devils
howling from the walls, he'll get infected,
like me, at least he should have a chance
to grow up normal, to earn some happiness,"
she'd chatter on, half the time crying,
half the time laughing so you couldn't tell
what state she was in except hysterical,
you could bet most times somewhat
hysterical come hell or high water
and you'd be right. The Greek, you know,

means womb-struck, or near enough.'

I looked at the painting again—the light
seemed to be dimmer, in the tomb-like room,
and in the gloom the figures had blended
with the background in a complex pattern.
A clown in the shade of a loquat tree looked up
from reading a book, a finger holding his place,
or perhaps pointing at a moral lesson
too finely wrought to read, posed
like an Elizabethan dandy. A spanner
poked from a pocket, a pair of spectacles
dangled from a chain.
'That's her boy-friend,
or a good likeness. A hippy mechanic.
A Buddhist text in one hand, a bottle
in the other. He said his Harley-Davidson
was his Poem of the Open Road. Dreck!
But that was her world, the Seventh Circle
of Bohemia, Reich the Priest of Orgasm,
Coltrane, coffee and Existentialism.
The theories! Everyone had one.
We drank, we danced, we talked till dawn.
They talked Karl Marx at me—me!
I knew Hegel like the back of my hand,
and Marx, Engels—"Know thine enemy!"

'Then she fell pregnant. Well, the father,
who was to say what was God's intention?

'I went to visit when the baby came,
at the "Hotel Methedrine", I called it,

a house full of ratbags and derelicts.
He thought the child was his, and I remember
thinking how slowly the truth would grow,
as he turned into a boy, then a youth—
"teenagers", they call them now—then
into a young man—by then the evidence
would be staring at him. What would she say?

'They had a party to celebrate,
a jazz group played in the studio
around an old Bechstein I had bought her,
and a foraging throng of babbling beatniks
spilled around and milled in the yard.
I was taken to the front room—bedroom,
cloakroom and parlour—to see the child.
The couple—how can I explain? The drugs—
forgive me, but you don't seem the type—
the effects of an excess of methedrine—
the speed was real speed in those days,
no horse tranquillisers then—
and real methamphetamine hydrochloride
has a number of peculiar side-effects,
apart from keeping you up till Doomsday
to hear the trumpet sound. Use it for long
and you're left in a state of alternating
brilliance and truly sickening depression
with paranoia smouldering around the edges.
It also eats your brain—actual holes,
big enough to push your finger through—
a medical student once—well, never mind.
It also makes you chatter like a parrot,
and it produces a relentless grinding

of the teeth, sleeping, waking and talking,
a grinding back and forth, back and forth . . .

'There they were, the parents, the loveliest
woman painter in the world, and that cretin
the trick motor-cyclist, smiling alternately
down at the baby, and up at me. The child,
having imbibed with his mother's milk
a love of peasant music, a savage temper,
and a fair dose of the booze and speed
that were always blended in her veins,
was smiling up at them adoringly,
its little gums grinding back and forth,
back and forth . . . it was horrible.
I went back to the party. I got drunk.
I threw up in the toilet. I went home.

'I need a coffee, something to clear my head,
what about you?' the Captain said,
and steered me to the lift. 'The espresso here,
marvellous stuff, cut it with a knife!'
The lift was mirrored on all sides,
so that we seemed a thousand strong,
a fourfold army of ourselves stretching
rank on rank into the glassy gloom.
We went down a floor or two—at least
the lift seemed to move downwards, meaning
we should have been moving deep underground,
but when I stepped out into the lobby
I caught a glimpse of the evening sky
through a distant window with red drapes—
sunset on the Harbour, molten light,

a motionless airship advertising
something—a book, a brand of beer.
The lift, the Captain's badly-fitting wig,
his strangled intensity, his crooked tale,
had left me feeling dazed and confused.

The Captain called a waiter over. 'Paul,
Paul,' he cried out, and laughed loudly,
and grasped the young man around the shoulders.
'What d'you think?' He displayed the waiter
like a farmer showing off a pig.
He pinched his cheek. 'Damn the Dentistry!
See a bit of life, work hard,
play like a possum, life won't wait.'
Under his rain of laughter the boy—Paul—
smiled cheerfully, and clasped his silver tray
across his belly. He was pale, plump,
and sweating slightly, with gold spectacles.
'Bring us something nice, a little spicy,'
the Captain ordered, and Paul beamed,
bowed quickly, and trotted to the kitchen.

'What could I do?' The Captain lit a cigar.
He sighed. 'Dentistry, his mother wanted.
Her teeth are giving trouble, but we already
have a good dentist, an angel of a man,
a Doctor Caisley. Let the boy do Medicine,
let the boy paint—God forbid!
from the mother—let him—what was it
Maugham said? A friend of his—a woman,
and a Devotee of the Master—asked
what should she do about her son,

keen to be a writer of some sort.
Give the boy a thousand a year—enough
to live on in moderate comfort—then
send him to Europe. That was Maugham's advice.

'Young Paul's been to Europe. Paris.
Rome. Couldn't stand a bar of it.
London? Hated it. California likewise.
Joined a band, gave that away.
Now he's in a monkey suit. I fixed it
with Papa Florenzini, the old man.
Be firm with the boy, I said,
I don't want a slacker for a son.
At least he'll learn manners, and restraint,
which is more than his mother ever gave him.'
He gave me a long look—'You've guessed,
I suppose—'
                    Just at that moment
Max's voice was heard, and soon the group
appeared around the door, arguing,
gesticulating. 'Captain, O My Captain',
Masterson called across the room, 'pray
do join us in a little snack!'

But it was this loose perambulating
group of pilgrims who did the joining,
rearranging chairs and moving things
until I was separated from the Captain
and our table was full to overflowing.
I loosened my tie—the place was crowded,
and a rich scent of cooking filled the room.

'Try the smoked eel,' suggested the Saint.
'Not as good as I've seen served
in a certain tavern in Budapest,
but passing fair.' Professor Flack beamed,
and his eyes flickered around the table.
'The retsina they serve here is remarkable,'
he confided. 'In Macedonia, during the War,
I tasted the very same brew. Tinted
the faintest shade of pink, like the dactyls
of rosy-fingered Dawn herself. Delicious.'

Florenzini's was famous for its fish
and soon a great platter of lampreys arrived.
They were exclaimed over and quickly dispatched,
and Paul and his cohorts scuttled back and forth
like slaves at some Pyramid of Hunger.
The retsina, brought in tall jugs,
washed down the courses of fish that followed
one on the other—an *Aguilla in Tiella*
al Piselli—eel in green peas, a specialty,
then salt cod in raïto, civet of inkfish,
and a tiger prawn salad.
'Max, you were speaking
of Stella,' said the Captain, when the table
had quietened down and the *granita de caffé*
had arrived. 'You were speaking of Love,
but Hunger claimed us. We were dispersed,
like the Jews, a diaspora in Florenzini's.
Now we're gathered again in the name
of Discourse. We are fed, and ready.'

Max—always the stage-manager—carefully

applied the flame of his platinum lighter
to a Cocktail Sobranie—gold-tipped,
lilac-tinted paper, a scented blend
of Egyptian and Greek Xanthos tobacco—
blew the smoke in a wreath around his head,
and launched himself on the slow, dark
waters of reminiscence.

'Stella's husband,
Harry, his name was, puffed up,
arrogant, sick with hate. The sin of anger.
I killed him. God help me,' Max said.

During the long, cold hush that followed,
I noticed that the restaurant was almost
empty. What time was it? Late.

'Not meaning to. Not consciously, that is.
But who knows? I was a demon at tennis,
fit, not like you see me now.
His father had died at forty, bad heart,
collapsed in the prison yard, chopping wood.
He'd been in jail for just on seven days.
Embezzlement, fraud, something to do with
business, dishonest, the partner suicided.
The son, growing up, you can imagine,
ashamed, determined to make up the lack,
wash away the stain. What went
through his mind, when he was growing up?
He turned out a bully, he was built
like an ox, he met any challenge
head-on, angry, determined to win.'

Max took a draught of the retsina.
The moisture condensing on the jug
had made a ring of water on the tray,
and he traced a pattern with his finger.
'A heatwave—seven days of temperatures
over the century, it burnt your skin
even in the shade, a breath from Hell.
I challenged him, a game or two of tennis.
After an hour he was losing badly.
The heat was boiling up from the court,
asphalt, almost melting in the sun.
You could smell the hot tar. "Harry,
let's call it off," I said. His face
was a sick colour, a blotchy mix
of grey and pink. "Damn you," he said,
"play on, damn you, you bastard."
He knew about me and Stella, you see.
What could I do? "Leave it," I said.
The courts were on the outskirts of town,
behind a half-acre paddock of derelict
trucks and broken-down bulldozers
that Harry had picked up at an army sale
and hoped to make a killing on, one day.
The courts were empty in the heat. "Harry,
leave it," I said, "we can pick it up later."
But he played on until he thrashed me.
I let him beat me. Why not?

'I'd won, hadn't I? I drove him home,
and left him at the front gate. "I'll
call you tonight," he said, gasping.
"Swine like you have to be taught a lesson."

What did he mean? What was he planning?
Revenge? God knows. I drove off.
He never made it to the house. The boy,
his son found him face-down on the path,
the brick path, about an hour later,
when he came home, he'd sneaked out,
he should have been at home practising
his scales, he would have heard his father cry
out, before he fell, out of key,
a sound never written in a music book.
He could have telephoned the ambulance.
The doctor, the paddles, the shock—
the subjunctive mood, it's full of pain.
"If only . . ." and so on. And so forth.
Time is one-dimensional, a one-way street.
Once a thing is done . . . The poor kid.
He'd sneaked away, he was smoking
and looking at a dirty magazine
behind the shed, cruel innocence,
who is to blame, the heart? The faulty genes?
His dad's father cheating on his friends?'

Max stared at his drink. I could hear
a clock ticking somewhere. Sandra stirred
and spoke in a whisper, so quietly
that she might have been speaking to herself.
'What happened to the boy?' she asked.

'Poor little bugger,' Max said.
'He went strange after that. I tried,
I tried to bring him out of himself,
but it didn't work. I took him fishing.

I gave him a camera, I taught him
photography, he took pictures of things
dead, run over, a cat crushed
and left by the road, fish heads.
I bought a gun, took him hunting rabbits,
but that was no good, he'd turn and fire
into the trees, he'd empty the magazine.
I was afraid he'd do something terrible.
The more I tried to reach the boy, the more
he pulled away. Stella was the same,
she put up the shutters.' Max frowned,
a plaintive tone gave his voice an edge.

'She took the boy off on a trip,
one of those bridge club cruises
you read about, where fifty rich people
learn the game from bridge professionals
cruising in the Caribbean. Stella
knew some guy, so she got the trip
teaching people bridge, she was good,
and I guess they sympathised. Fine.
She wanted to forget, she said, the boy
needed a chance to grow, to get away.
Next thing I know I get a letter.
She's met this fellow in Miami,
a businessman, a rich card player,
real estate dealer, speculator.
She was infatuated, I could see that,
poor Stella half mad with grief,
the opportunities for error, well,
there's no need to fill in the picture.'

Max topped up his glass and drank.
'I happened to be in Southern California
some time after that, on business,
so I called on the happy family.
The boy, he'd picked up an accent,
talked like a Yank, it was embarrassing.
To me, that is; not the new father,
he said he liked the kid to call him Pop.
They'd gone there from Miami for a reason,
to catch the boom, Stella said, land,
a real estate explosion in the making,
the way she talked, like a wave, a tremor,
if you were sensitive you felt it coming,
like a train deep beneath the earth,
the crash of steel cars colliding
underground, and in that maelstrom
vast financial forces could be tapped,
and a tidy profit plucked from the wreck.
Don't you want the boy to have a chance,
she asked me, good schools, a job?
A fool could make a fortune in a week,
the new husband chuckled, no problem.
Stella looked terrible, I could see it
if no one else wanted to, apparently
the husband drank, and naturally Stella
hated it—we found ourselves alone
for a moment and I took the opportunity
to pour my heart out to her as I had
so long ago—Leave him, Stella,
my darling, I said, and come with me.
She used to have an understanding nature,
but America had changed all that;

she seemed self-centred and ambitious.

'She couldn't break away, it was clear;
she knew she'd made a terrible mistake,
but admitting to it was another thing,
she pretended she was mad about him—
his crude manners, his moods—and it seemed
she had to match his drinking with her own.
I couldn't stand to see her like that—
trembling, red-eyed, bitterly
unhappy—at one point she tore off
a bracelet I'd given her before,
when we were in love, and flung it away.
I got filthy picking up the stones
where they'd fallen underneath the fridge.

'Well, her husband—Stanley was his name,
a stocky, hearty fellow, well built,
thick hair on his arms and shoulders—
Stanley was badly short of staff
down at the office, and as it happened
I knew how to sell a block of land.
I said I'd help out—What are friends
for?—and Stella needed some support,
to be frank, to help her face herself
and her responsibilities—the kid,
for example, was turning more American
every day, the less attractive qualities,
I mean—he was keen to make a million
before he turned twenty-one, trading
used earth-moving gear, tractors,
trucks—and this from a young man

who used to play the cello like an angel.
If only God had granted me a little
time, that's all I wanted, time . . .'

Now it was the coffee he gulped at.
He showed his teeth, discoloured by tobacco,
in a snarl like a yawning dog.
'I felt like a sucker,' he complained.
'All that love I'd given her, it didn't
mean a damn thing. I'll admit
I got upset by some remark of Stella's,
I should have kept calm, the doctor said
not to get angry, my heart was bad,
deep breathing, count to ten, relax,
but who cares, it was broken anyway.
Something Stella said. I saw red.
Hell, she was a lovely woman, even
shrieking like that—"Go!" she said,
"Go away!"—I still have the scratches,
look—' he showed us his neck— 'but
it was the drink speaking, and the heat—
it could get so dry in that house,
an electrical feeling like a migraine,
a silent, stealthy heat, the desert
gaping beyond the patio, and the wind,
the Santa Aña wind that used to blow—
something she said, I don't remember,
I think I broke a few things, Hell,
I was always clumsy, and then—my heart—'

He reached into the air with his hands,
pawing, sweeping an unseen treasure

towards his chest. His face was flushed and damp,
he seemed on the edge of an emotion
that might crush him if he let it
take one more inch of his body—

'My damned heart slammed to a stop!
The pain! Everything black! The next thing,
I wake up in a room like a morgue,
terrified, dry mouth, nausea,
plastic tubes coming out of me,
and pain—a shark tearing at my chest,
and a debt—my God, American
hospitals, thirteen thousand dollars—
When I came to, I phoned around—
Stella had disappeared, moved again,
back to Miami. The Californian
real estate deal had fallen through
badly, it turned out, a severe
miscalculation on Stanley's part,
and the three of them had shut the shop
and shot through with a half million bucks,
and I had a State Fraud One-O-Seven
hanging over me, all for helping
Stella's husband sell a block or two
of rather dry country in Nevada,
what should I know about Nevada law?
They repossessed the trailer home, the car,
a ring I'd bought for Stella—gone, the lot.

' "Lay down your burden," the orderly said;
"agree with everything the doctor says
but just don't lift anything heavier

than a highball and you'll be fine."
I did some listening, not to doctors,
what would they know in the area
of coronary attacks? Sure, they study,
they have a licence to take your money,
but watch them tour the wards—a nod,
a smile, they feel your pulse, they feel
your wallet, kiss my arse and wave goodbye.
But the nurses and the orderlies,
they *live* with death day and night,
they see every little symptom,
they wheel in the living and they
trundle out the bodies. Look at this!'

Here Max tore open his shirt
and bared his midriff. The sudden gesture
took me by surprise. I had half
doubted his story, but here was evidence—
a scar like a giant zipper that tore
from the exact centre of his chest—
it was heaving, he was gasping for air—
down and under his ribs, to disappear
behind his back. 'Thirteen thousand bucks!

'I lost Stella, I died on the table.
What's it like in Hell?' He laughed at his joke.
'I only saw the ante-room, the lobby.
Decorated with old *National Geographics*
and dirty magazines with torn covers.
Hey, I'm kidding! What should I know?
I'm alive, and poor Harry's dead.
That's all. For what? For nothing.

Look at me, a bankrupt. But alive.'
He laughed—a high, wheezing sound,
as though some invisible assailant
had their hands tight around his throat.

'For nothing, all that suffering,
the bridge games I could never follow—'
he was struggling to form the words—
'the wind, the rain pouring on the roof
of Harry's old Nash—' here his tale
foundered—'the kisses, the cheating . . .'
A handkerchief came out, and mopped his face.
His chest was heaving, and I realised
he was crying in great deep gulps,
shuddering, but quietly, like someone
not wanting to be overheard.
'Where's the Men's Room? I gotta go.'
Sandra directed him. The spell was broken.

Flack went out for cigarettes. The Captain
talked quietly to Sandra by the door.
Paul joined them, and the older man
put his arm around their shoulders. I was
thinking what an odd trio they made,
when the Saint, quite close to my ear,
startled me.
'Do you know the motives
that Adler ascribed to the compulsive
fantasiser?' he asked, in his careful,
hard-to-place accent. 'Of course not.
Few people read him any more.
The high-flying eagle is a moth-eaten

old bird now, asleep on his perch
in some dim museum. This was an early
formulation—later he recanted,
but mistakes—as the Master reminds us—
are much more important than they seem.
Adler of course was a disciple
of the Great Sigmund, but who could stand
the heat of that blaze for long? And Freud,
such a Jealous Father, always driving
the fledgelings from the nest. Personally
I have always felt that intellectual
pursuits are vain. Not in themselves,
but because they are so obviously
a long way around, an unnecessarily
circuitous route to the satisfying
of the real needs—Greed, Desire.

'So the greedy Max weaves his nets.
And we are all departing now,
I think. The rain has stopped.'

The Captain drew me aside as we were leaving,
and led me to a painting hung high
at the end of the hallway, past the lifts.
'Look at this before you go. Tell me
what you think.' I looked, and wondered—
did I know the artist? A large oil,
strongly coloured, framed between a pair of
crimson drapes—a water scene, the late
afternoon light spilling across
a bay—boats—a large cargo ship,
and on the funnel was the emblem

of a publishing conglomerate,
one of the Captain's better business ventures.
The sky was heaped with golden cloud, and thronged
with aircraft, mostly 1930s biplanes,
and a distant decorated zeppelin.

'It's real, but emblematic too,' he said,
'it all means something else. Art makes
life worth living. So does passion.
Not sex—I mean the whole thing.
So does a stock exchange collapse.
Why do we speak in riddles? That's the question.
Unanswerable. Let's catch the others.'

As we stumbled down the rain-wet steps
of Florenzini's, murmuring in small
intent groups, the last rays of the sun
slanted across the street and lit the park.

BREATHLESS

BREATHLESS

It was an autumn evening, after a meeting
at Masterson's; four of them stood on the steps.
'I could do with a meal,' Hunter said;
he really wanted to talk more with Sandra.
'Florenzini's is the only place in Sydney,'
proclaimed Lovelock, a young painter
with thick red hair. 'What do you think?'
Sandra—thirties, smart, a pretty blonde,
wearing a plaid skirt and sky-blue top—
agreed enthusiastically: 'It's just the place.'
So they set off down the darkening street,
with Sandra and the painter striding ahead
and Hunter and Mr Tennyson Lee following.

If you'd told Hunter he'd spend that night
in the arms of a self-confessed murderer,
drinking gin and listening to Billie Holiday
singing the blues, he wouldn't have believed you;
but as it happened, that's where he ended up.

Around them the Australian economy staggered
under the assault of various foreign banks,
and crowds of workers lately turned into their
doppelgängers shopped angrily, consuming
what they produced in a different incarnation.
It seemed that the contradictions engendered
by the anomalous life-style of the urban worker
were producing a kind of psychic acid,

and it rained around them in a thin mist.
'What do you think of this dago dive,
Florenzini's?' Lee asked Hunter,
as he kicked aside a small terrier
tugging on a tartan lead. Its owner shrieked
and shook a fist, but was soon lost behind
in the tumult of confused but purposeful shoppers.
'Are you fond of the Italians, Mr Hunter?'
'I hardly know the place,' Hunter yelled
over the thunder of a passing truck.
'I haven't seen much of Sydney since—
oh, ages ago. I'm a bit out of touch.'

Crossing against the traffic, Sandra stumbled
in her high heels, and a motor-bike
almost knocked her down. She shouted
at the rider's disappearing back—the noise
of the revving engine made it hard to hear
exactly what she'd said, but for a moment
Hunter thought she'd shouted an obscenity.

At Florenzini's they huddled into a booth
near the front, where they could look out
through the misted glass at the pedestrians
struggling in loose herds through the rain.
The restaurant was old and dimly lit,
the walls covered entirely with paintings—
all badly executed, Hunter thought,
student work, apparently, from years ago—
and the crockery was chipped and motley:
'Newcastle Hotel', said a dinner plate,
and a cup and saucer claimed the parentage

of the Victorian Government Railways.
They ordered bowls of the thick spaghetti
the place was known for, and a bottle
of the appropriate cheap red, then,
when that was gone, a bottle or two more.

'I think Masterson's a bully,' Lovelock
muttered eventually, wiping the gravy
from his beard. 'Did you notice the way
he hammered Flack, and poor old Sturgeon?'
Lee pounced. 'Rubbish! You speak, my friend,
the product of the bull. Masterson?
A bully? Cruel? Quite the opposite.
He succeeds like a lawyer, by pleading.'
'You've both got him wrong,' Sandra put in,
stripping off her powder-blue cardigan.
'God, it's hot.' She shook her blonde hair
loose. At thirty she'd gone back to study
something vaguely masculine at night,
Hunter remembered—building, or town planning—
and though her voice had a breathy edge
she spoke confidently. 'No, Masterson
is a leader, but his strength is hypnotic.
He hasn't turned his magnetism on you yet.
He can see you're not ready to receive
his insights. Like the wise rhinoceros
in the fable, who refused to be hurried,
he's biding his time. When that time comes
he'll turn the power of his gaze on you,
and you'll wilt.' She laughed suddenly,
making fun of them, Hunter felt,
though he couldn't quite see the point.

Lovelock fiddled with his meagre moustache.
'Rhinoceros horn,' he said, 'now there's
a kick. There's a drug to stir your blood,
and turn your superego to a heap of jelly!'
'So you've tried the famous rhino horn,
my friend,' said Lee. 'Was that during your
East African sojourn, the elephant safari
you spoke of so eloquently today?'
'Rhino horn? Is that like cocaine?'
asked Sandra, in what Hunter realised
was a faint American accent. Why hadn't he
noticed it before? 'I'd love to try some.
Do you sniff it? How is it prepared?'
She seemed to be leading Lovelock on.
'Powdered rhino horn, like a certain gland
of the marmoset and a poisonous secretion
of the Indonesian Coral Whelk, is an
aphrodisiac, Sandra,' intoned Lovelock.
'I'm not quite sure that your background
has prepared you properly for its effects.'
There was something pompous about his manner.
Hunter noticed Sandra's mouth tighten.
'What would you know about my background?'
she whispered angrily. Lovelock went on:
'I believe in trying all experiences,
so of course I've dabbled with rhino horn.
Once, on the Gold Coast of Africa—'

'Your philosophy cannot be so
immature,' interrupted Lee.
'Trying all experiences, indeed!
What of the experience of ingesting

cement, pray tell? What of leprosy?
And any fool knows that rhino horn
is not an aphrodisiac. But enough of this.
Sandra,' he said. 'You've hardly eaten.
Can I order you a second course?
There's an old saying, that a man—or
a woman, I presume—should eat like a king
in the morning, like a prince at midday, and
like a beggar at night. And look around you—
the women eating like goldfish at all times,
and the men like a pack of wolves. I'd be charmed,
my dear Sandra, if you'd try some
Drunken Beef with me. It would do your blood
a power of good.' Sandra blinked.
                                        'Some what?
What did you say? Did he say "Rump Beef"?'
Lee laughed politely, and touched her arm.
'No, my good lady, I said "Drunken Beef",
a specialty of Su Shih's Chinese Restaurant,
whither I propose to take you. This
Italianate monstrosity is overpowering,
it's too much for a tender soul like mine.'
They looked around them. Florenzini's was
hot, smoky and full of shouting customers.
Hunter felt that he was getting drunk.

'I don't know about this Chinese restaurant
of yours,' Lovelock said, 'but "Drunken Beef"
is in fact a Japanese dish. De Quincey
got it wrong too, but he had the excuse
of being stoned on opium. He claimed
he saw it in a vision—a boiling vat of

buffalo and beer, attended by Malays.
In fact it's a regional speciality of Kobe,
on the Southern Island of Japan.'

'As usual,' Lee said, 'through your arrogance,
you have misunderstood. We have a saying:
"Those who speak cannot listen, those who
listen do not speak." So listen, please.
Yes! I have been to Honshu in Japan where
the famous Drunken Beef originated, and there
watched the unfortunate animals fed, and later
eaten of their flesh. They are nailed firmly
by the hooves to a floor of oak planks,'
embroidered Lee—Sandra went pale—
'and force-fed a blend of corn meal,
Irish stout, and the finest Calvados,
the famous apple brandy of Normandy.
When the wretched animal is plump enough,
it is slaughtered by a Shinto priest,
the meat is hung for the ritual period,
a lunar month, and embalmed in rice vinegar.
It is seared lightly, and devoured as warm
as the Apostle Luke's faith, as it were.'

'By the hooves!' exclaimed Sandra. 'By the
hooves! Oh, those orientals are so cruel—'
Realising her blunder she went red,
an attractive flush spreading quickly
up from her neck, which was ornamented
with a string of peach-tinted pearls.
'Oh, fuck—I didn't mean . . . that is,
the Chinese, they're not the same at all . . .'

‘As you infer,’ said Lee quickly, ‘the Japanese
are different from the older Asiatic races.
The Chinese, among whom I number
some of my ancestors, are a subtler
and less warlike people. In the East
the Japanese are noted for the cruelty
of their women—a canard, I might add.
There’s a folk tale I heard once
in a bar in a jazz club in Shanghai,
involving the faithless wife of a Japanese
rice merchant. This female oaf, one night
during a terrible storm, took into her house
a half-drowned sailor. Her husband was away
in the capital dealing in rice, tired
and footsore—’ He broke off here, remembering
the thrust of Sandra’s original complaint.
‘But you mustn’t labour under the delusion,
my distressed and slightly inebriated lady,
that it matters a whit to the hapless beasts
to have their feet fastened to the floor.
Hooves are—how shall I say—integumental,
like the toenail. Done with care—or,
in the case of the Japanese ranchers,
if we can call them that, with skill,
the neighbour of care—performed with a modicum
of skill, it causes the beast no pain at all.’

‘You’re full of bull,’ said Lovelock angrily.
‘I don’t believe a bloody word you say.
Show me this restaurant.’ They both stood,
Lovelock knocking over his empty glass.
‘Follow me,’ Lee said, and in a moment

they had gone in a swirl of coats and scarves.

Hunter reflected sadly on the bill.
'Let's finish that bottle,' he said.
'I doubt they'll be back. If they do find
Su Shih's they'll try the Drunken Beef,
and if they don't they'll either quarrel further,
or find a bar and try to patch it up.'
Sandra nodded, and he noticed she was upset.
'What's the matter?' he asked.
'Oh, nothing,'
she said, blowing her nose. 'I've been taking
various things to fix a sinus headache,
and they always make me feel a little flaky.
Besides, it's that time of the month.
All I wanted was a bit of fun,
a glass of wine, a story, conversation,
something to remind me that I'm human.
And now, a fight, a quarrel, and it's over.
I thought I'd left all that behind.
But you never can, isn't that right?
You've been around, I can tell.
Oh, the things a person can survive, it's
extraordinary, the papers wouldn't believe it.'

She rummaged in her bag and found a bottle,
and spilled a heap of pills onto the laminex.
They were brightly-coloured, like beads—
red and yellow ones, pale blue and black,
clear capsules filled with crystals,
a scattering of apricot tablets.
'Eenie, meenie, miney, mo,' she said,

and swallowed one, washing it down
with half a glass of wine. 'You see, when Derek—
Mr Lovelock—talked about his brother
being killed by an elephant in Africa—
that's what threw me, I guess, because
I had a brother, and he died too—
and it was my fault, because of a pizza!'
She swept the scattered capsules into her bag
and snapped it shut. Hunter was intrigued.
'I thought you said you were an only child,'
he said, 'earlier this evening—'
'Yes,
that's true, but I also had a brother.
But not any more. I've lost—I've lost—'
She faltered, stopped, and started again.
'Sometimes I think I'm another person,
so much of my life has disappeared.
We were living in the States then,
my dad took us there in the early sixties,
he worked for an oil company, in Canada,
then in Southern California.
I would have been . . . oh, twelve, I guess. Tony—
that was my brother—what a lovely guy—
Mom and Dad were out, and I asked Tony
to get us a pizza from the takeaway place.
Just down the street. He took the bike,
he had this big Harley-Davidson, God
what a noise it made, he used to
tune the engine in the yard and just sit
and listen to the sound, as though the bike
were saying something he could understand.'
She addressed her handkerchief, and went on.

'Just past the corner near the Dolphin Pool,
half way home, a Thunderbird hit him, some
rich kid whacked out on speed doing
ninety-five, the cops said, minimum, and
no lights. Poor Tony wasn't speeding,
just getting a pizza for his kid sister.'

'I'm awfully sorry,' Hunter said.
'Things are hard to take, at that age.'
He didn't want to change the conversation,
so he stopped there, and waited quietly.
He had a feeling there was more to Sandra
than she let you see at first—a strength,
a complexity of character, though each new
layer seemed to contradict the last.

'Mom and Dad never got over it. They broke up
two years later. Dad took to drink, I guess.
Mom took to men. And they weren't my parents,
not my real ones. That came out.
When Tony died, they told me. And later,
back in Sydney, I searched through the papers,
and sure enough, there was the story.
I was famous at the age of one.
Tot Survives Bizarre Tragedy, that's
what the papers said. And worse things.
My real parents were religious—
my father was a lay preacher with
the Plymouth Brethren—fundamentalists—
in a bush town miles from anywhere.
I guess we each have to find a faith
to fit our needs, like those molecules

that lock together in a certain way,
but what needs are satisfied by that
loony, punitive rigmarole?
I found out later that he thought
the baby—me—I wasn't his—
my mother had a lover, he believed.
Who knows? What does it matter now?
They were driving fast along a bush track
at dusk, going to some gathering,
the car full of bibles, the papers said.
And—I imagine this—arguing, fighting.
Around a bend, some timber-cutters
were jinking a large tree out of a gully,
and for a few minutes the steel rope
stretched out tight across the road.
Why wasn't there a look-out? Perhaps
there was, and they drove right through,
shouting, quarrelling. God knows.
The cable cut straight through the car,
decapitating both of them. I was
on the floor, asleep, in a basket
in the back seat. One of the papers—
I looked it up—said 'Father's Head
in Baby's Basket.' Can you believe that?
Isn't that sick? Who would write
a thing like that?

'So I was an orphan,
and my other parents chose me—*chose* me,
I wasn't just forced on them like now,
with adopted babies, incognito—chose me
from the orphans' home when I was one.
Like choosing a puppy, from the pound,

to save it from the needle. So, travel,
and America. And Tony's death.
He was an orphan too; his parents
had been killed in New Guinea, in the war.

'I hated America at first, when Tony died,
for what had happened. But I got used to it.
I found a sweetheart, a school romance.
We were too young, I know that now. But
how can you talk to a teenage kid? He was
weak, I can see that, but back then
all I could see was his brown eyes, just like
my brother's, and his kindness. We were happy,
for a while. We got caught up in that
hippie thing; smoked a lot of dope.
We both wanted a baby, but it seemed . . .
I couldn't have one, for some reason.

'Terry—that was my husband's name—he
got into bikes more and more, it was
a thing the Valley kids were doing then.
He'd dropped out of a couple of jobs—
computer programming, office work, then
working in a lumber yard, but he just
couldn't hack it, the routine, he said.
He joined a gang, the Wreckers; I had to
go along with it, I had nothing else,
did I? I had to follow where he went,
or I'd have lost him. Well, I lost him
in the end, anyhow.

'The gang leader
was a guy called Big Bob, a pilot,

someone said, in Korea, but he'd
dropped out, like the rest of us.
He had a silver medal that he wore
sewn onto his jacket, upside-down,
that he called his "dead-men money".
He'd been voted leader of the pack,
but you could tell he didn't want the job,
he liked to be alone. He had this hut
where he went fishing in the spring, and
lay about and read philosophy, he said,
but all I saw was fishing magazines.

'A year or so went by—you know, with bikers,
they say they're bad and violent, yet
all I can remember is the peaceful times,
talking, drinking beer, washing up,
like a summer camp, or a family
on a holiday that never ended.
And then Bob had this . . . accident.'
Sandra
swirled her wine, and stared into it
like someone who looks into a crystal ball
and sees something awful taking shape.

'We took our bikes out, six of us,
four bikes, for a picnic in the country,
and on the way home, in a valley
in the foothills of the Sierra Nevadas
we came across a flat stretch of road—
the lights of a homestead or two, no traffic,
and the highway like a strip of ribbon.
It was just on twilight, and Big Bob

stopped and looked back the way we'd come.
It was perfect for a game of chicken,
"Blue Angels", they called it—this
aerobatic trick they'd seen on television.
Two bikes would ride off a while,
a mile or so, while the others waited,
then they'd turn back, and both pairs
of bikes would race at each other like—'
she interlaced her fingers—'like so,
passing one between the other pair,
at ninety or a hundred miles an hour,
it takes a split second, and one mistake,
the slightest wobble—well, you can imagine.

'The darkness seemed to come on quickly—
it was cold, this was in the fall—
so we switched the lights on—"Go, Drake!"
says Bob, and the other bikes took off,
Drake on one, then Hogan and Maybelle,
and that hammering sound the motors make
faded away down the stretch of blacktop—
it grew quiet and peaceful, just our engines
turning over softly, and I heard a bird
whistling and chirping in the grass
at the side of the road. Terry and me
on one bike, Bob on the other, waiting,
the sunset like a big purple blanket,
the whole world fading into darkness.
You could see the stars coming out,
one by one, like lamps being lit.
The air was so clear, and it was so
lonely there, like the floor of heaven.

' "There they are!" said Bob, and revved up
and was gone in a scattering of gravel.
It took us five hundred yards to catch him.
"I'll take the centre," he yelled, "you
take the wing!" and he tilted the bike
to steer right between the pair of lights—
my God, the noise, a rolling thunder—
except, the headlights, it was a truck
loaded up with logs from Oregon
hurrying to get home to Oakland—
we heard the horn just before he hit,
that sound, like an animal in hell,
howling.'
                There were tears in her eyes,
just visible, but she blinked a few times
and they were gone. Hunter started to speak
then hesitated. What could he possibly say?

Sandra sniffed, then took out a compact
and looked at herself and pursed her lips.
'Worse things happen,' she said cryptically,
and snapped the compact shut.
                                        'Anyhow,
the second-in-command took over.
Drake, his name was, he was with us
the night Big Bob was killed. He was a
strange guy. Like Charlie Manson,
but not so sick or twisted, or as vicious.
Drake had a strange power over
men or women—anyone, it didn't matter.
Charisma, they call it. Even animals,
he could tame a Dobermann, just by

talking to it, real quiet, I saw him
do it, to a guard dog in a timber yard.

'Well, most of the gang were just
out for a good time—parties, drinking.
Drake was different, he had a purpose:
sex, drugs, Nazi insignia,
like a religion, only upside-down,
and he kept bullying and pushing.
He soon twisted the gang around.
Some left, the others who stayed,
lost people like Terry and me,
sadists like Hogan, and silly Maybelle—
we were a crew of losers—ragged, dirty,
our minds all slightly wrong.
I think it was the drugs that did it,
that sent us off the planet into space.
I know I'm a strong person, underneath,
but in those days I was out to lunch.
Maybelle disappeared for a week, one time
out in the desert, and came back crazy.
She'd picked up a rich old man,
some insurance executive from New Haven
who was holidaying for a while in Reno,
so she was staying at The Gambler's Rest,
a classy motel way out of town—she said
she was half-drunk and half-asleep
when a purple flash lit up the room,
flooding in through the windows, and
when she went to look, it was a spaceship,
and they took her aboard, and she passed out—
they wanted to breed with Earth people, these

things with large pale heads—so they
put Maybelle into a tank of fluid,
and wired her up, and took out her memories,
then put them back, with a new personality.
They carried out sexual experiments
while she was hypnotised, she said,
and taught her the language that they used
and the history of their planet, blah blah,
then sent her back to wait, among
the people of Earth. Imagine, a biker's moll,
chosen to be an alien John the Baptist,
to make straight the way, in California!
Oh, the things you believe! And Maybelle,
two or three times a day you'd catch her
with her head tilted on one side, like a bird,
listening—"How are things, Maybelle?"
I said once, and she answered: "I'm listening
to the voices in the radio, they're speaking
to me, not to you, so get lost!"
One time from the washing machine,
she heard them, one time in her jaw,
she cried out and said "My teeth are buzzing!
Stop it!" and it was Them again,
talking from a filling in her tooth,
babbling and chattering through the static
with baleful messages, and weird instructions.
Like one time they told her
to cut off her hair, and she did; one time
to fetch thirty pounds of chicken livers
from some bird ranch in Oregon—
God, the smell!—crazy errands like that.
When we laughed at the things she had to do—

biting all the dogs she saw, one day,
washing her hands twenty times, another—
she just shrugged and said: "They're testing me."
We believed it, or we went along,
what's the difference? We were stoned
most of the time, and aimless, or rather
running in a circle after Drake,
doing what he said—there was a lot of
nasty sex—well, I don't want to
talk about that—and a killing once,
at least Hogan boasted he and Drake
killed a member of a rival gang,
but they lied about so many things,
who knew the truth? Our personalities
had been . . . knocked a little out of whack.
I wouldn't say brainwashed, exactly,
but it was close, and we all felt the same—
breathless, waiting for something to happen
that would lift us right up into the air.

'Then the Trek. That's what he called it.'

Just then a waitress came up—'Excuse me sir,'
she said to Hunter, 'but we're closing up.'
Indeed, Florenzini's was nearly empty,
the last few customers gathering their coats.
Hunter paid the bill, and they left—
'There's a place down near the water, let's
get a coffee,' Sandra said—so they wandered
downhill though the rain-wet streets.

Two hundred years ago a creek bed

would have led them to the bay; now
tram tracks and cobbles buried under asphalt
led them under half-lit tower blocks
past locked trucks, cafés shutting up,
pawn shops and fire insurance offices
to the oily waters of the Harbour.

The crowds had thinned out, the streets were dark,
but they found a coffee shop still open
and took a small booth near the front.
They could see the Quay through the glass,
and the last ferries nosing in to dock
and rest on the black, rocking water.
The waiter, in a strange insistent voice,
asked if they wanted a coffee, or—
he spoke lower—or a 'Special Coffee'.
'Oh, the Special,' Sandra said brightly,
and he brought them something in a cup
that wasn't coffee, but a kind of liquor—
'Vermouth,' Sandra whispered, though it wasn't
any vermouth Hunter recognised—pungent,
dark, and sugary, like a mug of port.

'The Trek,' Hunter nudged. 'You were saying?'
'The Trek was Drake's idea,' she said.
'He called it his Life's Work, he spoke of it
in biblical terms, but when you looked at it,
we were just a pack of bikers on a run.
It wound across the States like a rattlesnake:
Las Vegas, Amarillo, Albuquerque,
Route Sixty-six in the sun
to Oklahoma City, then Memphis—

you could say it was a flight into Egypt—
so we ended up in Alabama.
Drake had spent his childhood there, an orphan,
in this big old house that used to be
a mansion, before the Civil War.'
Here Hunter went to say something,
but thought better of it.
                                        'Alabama,
but the backblocks,' Sandra continued.
'Dirt roads, rusting automobiles,
weeds thrusting up through everything,
scrawny chickens running through the grass—
so we ended up one evening
in the ruined garden of the place
where Drake had grown up. As a boy,
he told us, he'd found a tunnel
that led under the main house down
a hundred feet into a limestone cave,
and in a heap of rubbish and broken wood
he'd found an old diary, and a pistol,
and in the diary was a message, he said,
that seemed to indicate that a treasure—
money stolen from the Southern armies,
at the end of the Civil War—was deeper down,
behind a dynamited rock-fall.

'There were only three of us by then—
half the gang had got into a fight
in Memphis, and ended up in jail,
including Terry—well, by that time
Terry and I had broken up, Christ,
life was a mess—where was I?—

and Hogan had smashed a leg passing
too close to a circus truck in Texas.
So Maybelle and I were sitting there
in the dark, holding a flashlight,
an old sack full of detonators,
whisky, and a plunger dangling a wire
that threaded down into the labyrinth
where Drake was placing his explosives
to blow away the rock—forty-seven
sticks of gelignite—he was bright, Drake,
but twisted, and he had this obsession
about prime numbers—so, exactly
forty-seven sticks, no more or less.

It was gloomy in there under the moss
and the shadow of the trees; I was brooding,
listening to the crickets and praying
we wouldn't be discovered by the cops
when Maybelle tilted up her head
and said out loud: "*Yes, Master!*"
Well, I freaked out—"What the fuck
is going on?" I whispered, and she
stared at me with a crazy smile—
her eyes seemed to light up in the dark,
and I believed, then, about the aliens—
"Sandra," she said, "the waiting is over!
Now I know what to do! The plunger,
you have to push the blasting plunger
when They give me the signal. Drake,
They know him as the Enemy of Light,
he let Bob die that night,
we were with Drake when the truck went by,

we saw him guess—the dark, the headlights—
but he made us wait, hypnotised—
his number's Forty-Seven, of years
on the planet Earth, and Forty-Seven
murders among men, his life
has ravelled out its thread, and he shall die.
Wait!"—she tilted her head the other way,
and seemed to listen to the Harley-Davidson
parked beside her in the leaves, the metal
ticking as the engine cooled—and
in the bizarre fright of that moment
I knew Maybelle was right. She said
"*Now!*" and time disappeared, like a piece
clipped from a ribbon, between the Now!
and the plunger there was no time,
no moment of decision, nothing! Just
the handle going down, and a thump
from far off, deep under the ground.'

There was a long silence. Hunter heard
a fog-horn far out on the water,
and the swish of passing tyres on the road.
It had been raining; liquid pools of colour
cycled through green, amber, red, as
the traffic stopped and started at the corner.
The waiter brought another 'Special Coffee'
without being asked. The stuffy air
was full of smoke; Hunter's heart was pounding
and he felt out of breath.
Just as Sandra
started to speak again, the door banged open.

It was Mister Lee and Lovelock, arm in arm,
carrying a bottle each, and laughing.
Hunter noticed that Lee had a bandage
wrapped around his right ear, and Lovelock
looked rather bruised about the face.
'Su Shih is the name, the nom-de-plume,'
said Mister Lee, 'of a friend of mine,
a master cook'—Here Lovelock interrupted—
'Not of Drunken Beef!'—and Lee went on—
'Master cook, a poet, and a diplomat.'
They sat down, squeezing into the space
so that Sandra was pressed against Hunter.
She looked into his eyes. 'Hi,' she said.

A jukebox that Hunter hadn't noticed,
in a corner at the back, began a quiet
jazz trio piece. He felt strangely happy.
'When Su Shih's not cooking, he's
drinking,' said Lee, 'and all the while
composing poems. Here's a lovely one—
please excuse my feeble translation:

The Harbour flows always to the East.
Its waters have drowned many lives,
Many sailors, poets, and gentlemen.
However sad, the waves keep flowing.

Perhaps these sentiments are silly,
And I am foolish, with my grey hair.
Life passes like a dream. So I drink
To the Harbour, and the Moon, this wine!'

Sandra laughed, her face to the light,
a full clear laugh that gave Hunter
a catch in his throat. Lee opened the bottle
and poured their glasses full. 'To good cooks,'
Lee said, and they drank. Hunter
put his arm around Sandra's shoulder.
The brandy had a sweetness, and a bite,
and a faint sparkle on the tongue.

Sandra raised her glass. 'Here's to
the sailors, the poets, and the gentlemen,'
she said. They drank again. The music
seemed to slacken its tempo, the drums
pulling the bass back, and then the bass
slowing, lifting the piano's embroidery

the way a wave might raise a line of bubbles
into a brief rippling crest of foam—
so thought Hunter, tasting his drink—
out across the cold moonlit waters
of the Harbour, where the last ferry,
its motors turning slowly, made for home.

RAIN

RAIN

Part One

'We went to America,' Kathy said.
'Colin was painting well then, and he was
on the edge of a breakthrough, he said.
Breakdown was more like it. He was drinking,
smoking a lot of dope. He'd sit on the floor
and stare at his work, and talk about his soul.
Why are men full of shit? He painted
big canvases, twelve feet across,
red, black and purple zigzags,
then he'd blacken them with a blowtorch—
trying to face up to the Americans,
he said. The way he talked about it,
it was like a boys' competition
down at the bottom of a schoolyard,
kids punching each other on the arm,
proving they could take the punishment.
You know, with Jackson Pollock, that
investment in the ego—prove yourself,
throw your soul onto the canvas,
one false step and you're a phoney.
But that's bullshit. You can make
as many false steps as you want;
if a piece doesn't work, you just
throw it out, or scrape it back
and paint something better over it.'

It was a lovely spring morning. We were

enjoying the breeze at the front of the ferry.
The light went down into the water
then it reflected off the sandy bottom
and glinted pale green through the waves.

'We were going to cafés in the Village,'
Kathy was saying, 'and reading books—
Action Painting, poetry, the Beats,
the Existentialists—popular philosophy
seemed to be obsessed with the arts then—
apart from the native consumer philosophy
that polished every American artefact
and made it glow with reflected money—
and every trend had a capital letter.
Colin said he had to get drunk to paint,
to see his own soul truthfully,
so he could wrestle with it, he said,
late into the night. You know, he slept
eight hours just like any office worker,
except he organised it so he slept
ten in the morning through to six at night.
People thought he was so full of fire
that he went without sleep. Huh!
Well, he liked to give that impression.

'What did I feel about New York?
I can't sort it out. It broke me.
It made me into an artist. I don't know.
I still have a lot of hostile feelings.
It's like advertising—of course it's
necessary, and often it adds flavour
and colour to things, but at the same time

it's obviously made up of greedy lies.

'I'd been fascinated by photography,
how a snapshot can freeze a scene
and turn a piece of three-dimensional
coloured, moving reality, full of sound,
scented, tinted with emotion and anger,
into something flat and motionless,
silent, permanent, like an art print,
and show you things you couldn't really see,
tiny details, the blur of frozen movement,
an expression that flitted across a face.

'That had been my major project
at art school, before I met Colin
and dropped out. I took it up again
in New York, just photographing people
on the street. I rigged up a darkroom
in the bathroom; everybody does.
It never gave me the results
I wanted—solid tone, clean prints—
I was always having to pack it up
so we could use the bathroom, and the air
was full of dust. In a darkroom
it's not the light that gets to be a problem;
you can work at night. No, it's the dust;
lint from towels, dust in the air,
dandruff, grit—it gets on the negatives
while you're printing, and the prints come out
with big white spots all over them.
But I managed. The work kept me sane
when things got bad—and they got bad—

and it reminded me of who I was.
I was disintegrating, otherwise.

'I drank a lot at first. I think
it helped me to cope, or at least
that's what I believed at the time.
Some of the people you meet—artists,
dealers, artists' wives—those people
were competitive. That was their style.
New Yorkers have a tendency to see
their worst faults as virtues—I guess
if you were one of those piranhas
and had to look in the mirror every morning
you'd gas yourself. So they'd developed
elaborate theories about how vital
competition was—competition, the essence
of petty capitalism, for God's sake,
not even monopoly capitalism, let's get
our focus set at the proper level,
we're dealing with the *petty* bourgeoisie—
how it separated the sheep from the goats,
artists from weaklings, men from boys—
they didn't mention women or girls—
and you'd hear them talking late at night,
high on speed, smoking the cigarettes
that Albert Camus actually used to smoke,
or so someone said who'd been to Paris,
arguing that the spotlight of fame
lit up the peaks, that fashion helped us all
to focus on the very best work,
without wasting time ploughing through
all that second-rate stuff. The critics

would do that. Shark eat shark, it was
a kind of Darwinism they were advocating.

'I had the kid to worry about—a big city
is no place to bring up a five-year-old.
But we found a school that Timmy liked—
at that age you adapt, he made friends,
and I'd take him early every morning—
I had to be up at six to do that,
get him ready, take the bus uptown,
so I had regular hours, of a sort.
And I'd shop, and work from nine to two
in a typing pool. We needed any money
I could bring in. I wasn't paid well.
I couldn't get a work permit,
so I wasn't officially supposed to work
at all. I was being exploited,
but we had to eat. What the hell.

'In the afternoons I'd collect Timmy
and take him to a park uptown
for a glimpse of grass and the ducks—
he used to love the ducks—then I'd
bring him home, and clean and get dinner.
Colin would be out at the Cedar Bar
drinking and arguing, or asleep,
or just away somewhere in the Jungle.
We called New York the Jungle.
Timmy would tell me about the things he'd done
at school. In a way it was a peaceful life,
if I'd been able to step back from things.

'We were young, and we certainly weren't rich.
Colin had just won a landscape prize,
and it seemed a lot of money at first.
But things are so expensive in New York.
He gave himself a year to make it
in the States, and it grew clear
as the last few months leaked away and
the bills mounted up, and the money went,
that he wasn't going to make it at all.
I felt terrible—for all the phoney talk
he really suffered, and he went through hell.
He'd swallowed the whole competitive myth,
and now he was at the bottom of the pile,
eating shit.
'About that time
an art dealer took to calling around.
He liked Colin's work, and my photographs,
he said he'd do a joint show in the spring.
He advanced us some money. Then some more.
He bumped into me in a bookshop one day,
and bought me lunch. And another time
at the laundromat, and we lunched again.
He was a nice guy, I thought; intelligent,
he read books, he was on the artist's side,
and he had that glow success brings.
And he used a lovely after-shave.
Oh, that's silly, I know, but scent,
the way a body smells, that's important.
I started seeing him from time to time.

'Well, don't look at me like that,
what was I supposed to do? Colin,

he was hardly speaking to me any more,
sunk in his drink and his marijuana
and his late-night painting binges.
I was as lonely as hell—America
can make you feel like you don't exist.
And Trent was so intelligent, so . . .
sophisticated, so full of enthusiasm.
You've got the same kind of confidence,
you know who you are, that's why
I like you.'
I didn't disillusion her.
Sure, my life was falling into a pattern.
I'd finished a degree in architecture,
and I'd spent two years in Thailand
working on a rural housing project.
I'd married recently—unhappily at first,
as it turned out, but that was my fault
for being headstrong about my career,
and I figured I could adjust and adapt.
In a month I was to start work with
a city firm, designing office blocks.
Yes, I should have known who I was.

'That's what I missed,' Kathy went on.
'Colin used to have it—that belief
in your work, in yourself, a zest—but
it got kicked out of him, worn away,
eroded. There's always someone else
better than you, younger than you,
someone with more energy, newer ideas,
more fashionable cigarettes, better
contacts, willing to compromise an inch

more than you. It really eats you up.
Colin was worn down to nothing. And
I must admit Trent was very generous.
We were broke, and he advanced us money.
And it was more or less understood
that if Colin made it, had a big show,
sold out, the money would be repaid.
If not—it was a casual arrangement.

'One night things got really bad—
Trent and I had drifted into the habit
of using cocaine from time to time,
at his place, when I'd put Timmy to bed.
He'd invited this other couple over,
and we drank some scotch, and did some coke,
and we all got pretty well stoned,
and the next thing I know I was involved
in this group sex thing, very unpleasant.
Don't look shocked; that was long ago.
Believe me, I was a different person. Jesus,
when I think of those manipulative bastards . . .'

Kathy was pretty, and when she was angry
a slight flush stole up her throat
and spread across her cheeks. Her eyes
were deep green with hazel flecks,
and they enlarged slightly as though
she were staring at something remarkable,
but she was only staring at her hands
as they slowly clenched and unclenched.
I noticed her skin was slightly freckled—
it seemed to match the eyes and auburn hair.

The unhappy emotions she described
made me feel close and somehow special.
Perhaps she had the gift of making anyone
she spoke to feel special, I don't know.
Her voice dropped perhaps half an octave
and an air of shared intimacy grew.
For no real reason, I remembered
taking my first puff of a cigarette—
you go dizzy, and your fingertips tingle.
Her arms were goosepimpled in the breeze,
and I felt an irrational urge to touch her
bare skin—just to brush her arm
lightly, with the back of my hand.
I felt myself go red suddenly,
and I turned away to look at the water.

Kathy had noticed nothing. 'Those
manipulative bastards,' she said again.
'When they left I got angry. I saw clearly
how I'd been used all along, set up—
even when he met me in the laundromat—
hell, Trent had his laundry sent out,
he was vain, such a pain in the neck,
he wouldn't be seen dead in a laundromat!
We had a fight, we were always fighting,
I asked him to drive me home—it was freezing,
a storm, and the rain had turned to sleet—
I remember the wipers on the windscreen
scraping back and forth through the mush—
Trent always drove fast—he had a Porsche,
what else?—I was crying and yelling,
he was laughing at me, I got mad—

I guess I must have hit him in the face.
We were doing sixty, at least, maybe more,
and in the wet the car skidded and rolled,
and kept rolling. I blacked out. Sometimes
I still have this dream, we're skidding,
the screech of metal scraping on the road,
and I'm reaching out for him, screaming—

'When I came to we were upside-down,
we'd gone through a metal fence and fallen
twenty feet into an excavation site.
My face was pressed against the roof,
the seat-belt holding me up, and Trent—
a metal pole had speared through the door
and through Trent's chest near the neck.
He was hanging there in agony,
clawing at it. He could hardly breathe,
and he made this horrible gulping noise,
over and over, trying to get air.
There was a stink of gasoline everywhere.

'Well, the ambulance, they cut us out
with jacks and metal cutters, they were wonderful.
They had to work fast, and they did.
I was just bruised, but they had Trent
full of drugs and serum while they worked.
By the time they got him to the hospital
he was in a coma. A lung was punctured
in the crash, the skull damaged, and the spine.

'I remember he said once the Porsche
wasn't quite up to his style, they just

didn't make a car flash enough. Well,
his style from then on was a wheelchair.
He couldn't remember anything at all,
not even me. Me! Jesus!
Can you believe that? Six months
we'd been seeing each other every Monday,
I thought I meant something to him,
and now I'm a zero, I don't exist,
he couldn't even remember my face!

'The cops found cocaine in his jacket,
traces, and searched the apartment,
and found more cocaine wrapped in foil
in the freezer, and marijuana under the bed.
He got six months in prison, a light sentence,
but it was the end of his art dealing days.
Finally his parents came and wheeled him back
to some hick town in Minnesota,
and no one ever saw him again.

'Oh God, look, we've arrived.'

I'd been so engrossed in Kathy's tale
I hadn't noticed where we were. I felt
quite light-headed and confused—
how was I supposed to react
to her story? Did she want sympathy?
She'd been working on her prints all night
getting ready for an exhibition,
and she'd taken lots of coffee and methedrine,
so maybe her emotions were a little skewed.

Jack and Colin joined us on the wharf.
We stopped off at a local shop and bought
bread and cheese and fresh ham for lunch
and walked around the shore to the houseboat.

It was moored in the shade of some trees—
the air was scented with lemon and eucalyptus—
close in to the eastern side of the island
in the shelter of a small bay. It was old,
but large and roomy, with a sundeck at the back.
The name 'Pequod' was painted on the bow;
a joke of Masterson's. He had money,
he often lent the boat to his friends,
and he'd fitted the place out comfortably—
there was a hi-fi with lots of records,
mostly jazz from the late fifties,
an old wind-up gramophone,
hot running water, plenty of books.
We had some lunch, and then a long nap.
Later we took a walk around the foreshore,
then wandered back to the houseboat
and played gin rummy on the deck
until it started to drizzle, and we went inside
for some hot rum and sandwiches.

Towards evening a storm came up
with a thrashing of leaves and heavy rain.
The six o'clock ferry failed to appear,
so we made up our minds to stay the night.
As dark came on it grew worse,
the wind knocking branches off the trees.

Jack opened a bottle of old bourbon
and we all had a drink before dinner.
I noticed Colin was drinking rather fast,
gulping it down quickly, and pouring another.
He knocked up a good sauce for the spaghetti
Kathy cooked, a kind of bolognese
heavily flavoured with garlic and black pepper
and some fresh basil he found growing in a pot
on the front deck of the boat. There was wine—
Masterson was proud of his well-stocked cellar.
We chose a strong burgundy-style red,
and ended up drinking half a dozen
between the four of us. It was a good meal,
with lots of talk and spirited argument.

After dinner Jack wound up the gramophone
and asked Kathy politely for a dance.
They circled gravely in the lamplight.
The rain had passed, and the night was still.
I had a coffee on the deck, and thought
how soon all this would be over;
the late nights, the talk, the drinking.
Soon I'd have a career to think about.
The music was plaintive country and western—
a blend of steel guitar and violins.
I recognised the 'Tennessee Waltz'.

We'd just organised ourselves for the night
and I was having a quiet drink with Kathy
on the deck, when Jack came out and said
that Colin had complained of feeling unwell.

We went inside. Colin looked awful.
'I should have left the drink alone,' he said,
articulating his words awkwardly. 'I'm sorry.
It was that last bottle of gin.' He laughed.
His face was grey. 'It's the tablets I'm taking.
You're not supposed to mix them with alcohol.'
Kathy gave me a look, and went to the kitchen.
I followed her. 'He's taken too much,'
she whispered angrily. 'It's morphine. I didn't
want to bring it up, but that's the problem.
He promised he'd leave the stuff alone,
at least for this weekend. Oh well.
What do we do? Keep him awake, I suppose.'
I couldn't think of anything to say.
I think I was shocked: about the drugs, or
about Kathy treating it so casually,
the two things were confused in my mind.
We went back into the living room.
'Keep him awake,' Kathy said. 'Just
walk him around a bit. He'll be right.'
'Did you hear that?' Jack said.
'Just keep awake, old son.'
I had a feeling he knew what was wrong.
Colin didn't reply. He'd fallen back
in his chair with his mouth open.
A string of spittle hung from his lips.
'I'll make some coffee,' Kathy said,
and went to the kitchen, tying on an apron.
'Let's get him up and moving,' I said.
I took one side, and Jack took the other,
and we began walking him around the room.
Colin's legs didn't seem very strong,

and he buckled at the knees once or twice.
Then he stumbled into one of the chairs,
so Jack rearranged the furniture
to give a clear passage through the room.
'Open the door,' I said, 'and take him
out onto the deck, then back again.'
'Oh dear, wait a minute,' Colin said,
and lurched for the railing. He threw up.
'Good idea, old son,' Jack said.
'Clear the stomach out. You'll feel better.'
He seemed to vomit forever, groaning
and heaving for breath between spasms.
Finally he wiped his mouth with his hand
and stumbled back into our arms.
'A touch of dry retching. Better now.
It's freezing, let's light a fire,' he said.
I don't think he knew where he was.
We took him back into the bathroom
and splashed cold water on his face.
'This is a waste of time,' Jack said,
drying his hands on a towel.
'It's no good. We've got to think of something
better to keep the bugger awake. Hey, Colin,
how are you? Are you awake?'
Colin mumbled. 'Listen,' Jack said.
'I'm going to tell you a story. A true story,
about a man who killed his pregnant wife,
a man who watched his enemy drown. So listen.
I want you to remember it, okay?
I'll ask you to repeat the main points,
so wake up and start listening. All right?'
'Sure, I'll listen. I'll remember.

My legs are wrong, they feel all rubbery.'
'Never mind your bloody legs. Just walk,
and listen.' Jack started talking;
and this is what he told us, as we stumbled
back and forth through the houseboat
from the kitchen to the half-lit living room
to the cool dark outside on the deck.

RAIN

Part Two

'When I came back from Korea,' Jack said,
'I looked around for things to do.
I didn't seem to fit in, somehow.
I tried selling trucks, then security work,
then I went to night school for a while.
I had a talent for journalism then,
taking photos, and writing up stories,
but nothing much ever came of that.

'Beth and I got married. The first year or so
was okay, but we got on each other's nerves
after a while, living in a small flat.
I had a feeling I was hemmed in,
my life was going around in circles.
I couldn't get a decent job, Beth
was thin and nervy. She was a city girl
originally, from Chicago, and she seemed
to suffocate in Sydney—though she said
it reminded her of home—it was the Harbour.
The only time she ever brightened up
was when we went for a picnic to a beach,
or for a weekend camping or fishing.
She was interested in intellectual issues,
but she liked to read about them alone.
She didn't make friends easily, I guess.
Finally she got a job writing stuff
for a magazine, a women's publication.

That brought in some money, but not much.

'Anyway, I hadn't done as well in Sydney
as I thought I might, so when I heard about
a job offer in Hartford, the country town
where I'd grown up, I jumped at it.
The local paper had changed from metal type
to photo-litho offset reproduction,
and the guy who'd made the photo blocks
was taking the chance to retire. He couldn't
cope with the new technology, he said.
He was just too old. They needed someone
to manage the darkroom and shoot the film
and develop the printing plates for the press.
I'd done some darkroom work, and I reckoned
I could learn the rest, so I took the bus
to Hartford and went straight to the owner,
a fellow called Bartlett. My dad had known him,
and old Bartlett remembered me as a kid.
"I'll take a risk on you, Johnny," he said,
"for your dad's sake." So Beth and I
packed our things and moved to the country.

'We rented a small house out the back
of the print shop, built from local rock,
a warm, honey-coloured sandstone.
Beth made it cosy in no time.
The first year there was no electric power
for one reason or another, but we had a stove,
an old wood-fuel thing—at six every morning
I used to get up and light it,
and put on a pot of coffee. For light

we had kerosene lamps that gave out
a soft yellow glow. Of an evening
Beth would sit at the kitchen table sewing
or working at a course she was taking,
in modern history and the labour movement.
Her cooking was wonderful—her family was Polish—
she'd cook dumplings, and potato cakes,
and beef stews, rich and full of spices.
I'd study up on my darkroom work,
but that didn't take much time.
Then I'd read—westerns, fiction, anything.
I was a great reader then—voracious.
I'd remember the flavour of a book—dry
and sharp, say, or heavy and simmering—but
the plot and what happened to the characters
would go right out of my head like smoke.

'For the first year my hands were full
picking up the trade. Old Bartlett
taught me all the photo-litho stuff.
He was well-read, and sharp as a pin.
He wasn't sentimental about type,
or the old Linotype machine.
"Noisy, poisonous bloody thing," he said,
when the truck came to take it away.
"Good riddance," he said, and that was that.
Once I had the job under control
I eased off a bit, and looked around.

'Hartford was a nice little town
a few miles inland from the coast;
small enough to be personal and friendly,

large enough to have a sense of activity.
People went to Sydney now and again;
there was a good high school and a branch
of a technical college, and a decent library.
Most of the money was in dairy farming.
There was an old sawmill outside of town.
A Bob Kingston owned the mill, a big man.
He had four brothers who worked there;
it had always been a family concern.
He owned the main hotel, and a hardware store.
I had some money, from my dad's estate—
he'd died soon after I was born—
and I started looking around to invest it.
I wanted to be part of the place again,
to feel I had a home, that I belonged.
Beth told me she was expecting a baby,
and the news gave me a bit of a shock.
I'd been used to weighing things up
with just my own fate in the scales;
now I saw things in a different light—
more long term. I saw how you had to
lay things down so they'd come into fruit
for someone else, miles down the track.
I bought some land on the outskirts of town,
and sold it six months later for a profit
to a fellow called Redding, an Englishman,
who set up an agricultural feed depot.
With the money I'd made I looked around
for something more substantial to invest in.
I soon saw Kingston was in my way.
Not deliberately, though he'd done things
against my father in the old days,

at least that's what Bartlett told me.
No, there was no reason, that was just
the way he was—arrogant, pushy.
If he saw that you were in his way
he'd just push you over, he wouldn't
ask you politely to step aside.
There was a block of land behind the pub
I wanted to develop as a garage.
I thought I could make some money on it,
and I knew it would work as an investment
for whoever set up shop there.
There were always trucks and tractors
needing to be fixed, and the other garage
was owned by a fellow who drank too much
and didn't seem to be that reliable.
When I put it up to Council for rezoning,
Kingston blocked it. No reason, he just
got the numbers up and blocked it.
Then he went around behind my back
and bought the land off old Willoughby.
He must have had some pressure there,
to push the old man around like that.
I had a contract and everything set up,
ready to sign, but Willoughby went yellow
and slithered out of it and sold the block
to Kingston, who left the land to rot
with castor-oil plants and stinking roger
growing up through the derelict cottage.
That really pissed me off, to be honest.
He didn't get any benefit out of it.
I faced him about the matter one day,
and he just laughed at me. He said

he didn't even want to talk about it.
"That's just business, young fellow,"
he said. "I'm bigger than you, that's all."
And that was the end of the matter
as far as Bob Kingston was concerned.

'I'd been playing around a little—hell,
the pressures of a new job, a new town,
my wife getting pregnant like that
without having planned anything properly—
well, there's no excuse, but there it was,
I was having this affair, with Paula,
she stayed in the hotel, the big one
on the riverbank that Kingston owned.
She worked as a barmaid part-time.
In the summer she flew a light plane
doing joy-rides at country shows,
stunt flying, that sort of thing.
She said she had some college diploma,
what she thought she was doing behind a bar
serving beer to farmers I don't know.
She had a kind of sullen air about her,
as though life hadn't treated her well,
but as far as I could see she'd done all right.
We met at the local dance—they had one
most Friday nights, a dinner dance,
you got to know people that way.
One night I gave her a lift home—
it was raining—it was late—well,
I don't have to explain how these things
happen—it's chemical, the scientists say,
the slightest perfume, some affinity,

I don't know—I parked behind the pub,
the rain was running down the windscreen,
that mournful song "Good Night Irene"
playing softly on the car radio—
when I hear that song I get the shivers—
I just turned to say good night to Paula,
there were raindrops on her eyelashes
and on her lips, and the next thing I know
we were kissing—that's all that happened
then, but it was magic, it was like a drug,
I had to see her the next day, and the next.
I began to avoid Beth—I felt terrible.
I made excuses to call in at the pub,
I got jealous if she spoke to other men—
God, it was Paula's job, to be friendly
with the customers, she was a barmaid, after all—
I had to see her, look at her hair, her lips—
not that anything happened, anything serious,
it was just a passion, we were acting
irrationally—I felt like a kid,
stupid, head over heels, ashamed.
Then Beth was killed. I killed her.'

Jack stopped here. 'Let him sleep,'
he said, and we dropped Colin on a sofa.
I was dizzy from walking in circles,
and bruised from bumping into furniture.
'I'm all right, Jack,' Colin said.
'A slight problem with the medication.'
He was awake by now. 'Ask me a question,'
he said. 'I remember everything.'
No one spoke. Had Jack killed his wife?

That's what we were all thinking.
'You got a job in Hartford,' Colin said.
'And there was a Kingston fellow, a bad type.'

'Help me bring in the coffee,' Kathy said,
and I went with her to the kitchen.
'What's this about his wife?' Kathy asked
in a whisper. 'You know him pretty well,
what's it about?' I knew him, but not well.
'How would I know?' I said. 'A wife—
I didn't even know he'd been married.
I don't understand what's got into him.'
Perhaps Jack was making it all up,
a kind of game to keep Colin awake.
I could see Kathy was still worried
about him—her mouth was drawn tight, and
her green eyes flickered about the room
in a distracted pattern. 'Hey, relax,'
I said, and put my arm around her shoulder
and gave her a hug. 'It's all right.'
'Sure,' she said, but she was still frowning.
We took the coffee out to the deck.
Colin was sprawled on a cane lounge.
'There's a giant fruit bat out here,'
he muttered, 'in the branches of that tree.'
'He'll be all right now,' Jack said,
and poured some bourbon into his coffee.
We sat there in silence for a while.
'I didn't kill Beth deliberately,'
Jack said. 'That's not what I meant.'
And—minus a listener, Colin
had dozed off—he went on with his story.

'One day I rented a small boat,
with an outboard motor, and I took her out
to a reef a mile or so offshore
where I knew we'd get good fishing.
We took a picnic basket—sandwiches,
cold lemonade, a bottle of beer.
Beth was the happiest I'd ever seen her;
she was expecting a baby, her courses
were going well, I had a job I liked.
Of course I was thinking of Paula, but what the hell.
There was a heavy swell from a storm
the day before, and the boat was moving a bit.
We caught a few nice bream, but
after an hour or so I could see
Beth was starting to feel unwell.

' "My dad owned a boat," she said,
"and he used to take us out fishing
on Lake Michigan, in the summertime.
I'd always get seasick from the movement,
but he never noticed, or seemed to remember.
Can we go in now?" A squall had come up
from nowhere, the sky had gone black
and the waves were getting big and choppy.
I started the motor and we turned for home,
and coming in across the bar, where the river
runs over a sandbank into the ocean,
the propeller caught in a patch of floating weed—
the outboard died, and the boat turned
side on to the waves. It was growing dark.
The water was very rough, green water
from the ocean churning with yellow mud

from the flooded river. It was pouring,
a cold, stinging rain. I grabbed the oars
and tried to turn the boat, but a wave
swamped us half full of water.
Beth was afraid, and for some reason
she stood up just as a big wave hit—
the boat tipped up and went over—
Beth took a terrific knock on the head,
and that's the last I ever saw of her.
I dived again and again—there was a rip
where the currents crossed, and I was swept
a mile down the beach. I woke in hospital.
It was two days before they found the body.

'It knocked me around, I'll admit that.
But I kept going. I drank a bit,
for a while, but I kept going. I had to.
Old Bartlett put up with a lot,
but in the end I pulled myself together.
I moved out of the house. I couldn't stand it;
everything I looked at—the kitchen,
the table where she'd worked at her studies,
the bed we'd slept in, even the scent
from the yellow roses she'd planted—all that,
it gave me the horrors and I couldn't sleep.
Then I began seeing Paula again.
I was lonely, you wouldn't believe how bad
the nights were, walking the streets
till the sun came up, talking to myself.

' "Let's go out to the silver mines,"
Paula said one day. I had a jeep,

a four-wheel drive, and we took that.
It was a lovely day, dry and clear.
We stopped halfway there for lunch,
and splashed in the river—it was cold,
flowing down from the high country,
water so cold it chilled your bones.
We had a beer, and ate some sandwiches.
It reminded me of my picnics with Beth,
and that got me down somewhat;
I'm not usually prone to depression.
And then there was something about Paula
that worried me. She acted like a loner,
strong and self-contained, but then she'd soften,
she'd go passive, and she seemed to invite
a man to be brutal with her, as though
she wanted punishment, and in reply
just a sulky stare. It was exciting,
I won't deny that, but it felt wrong.

'We drove further into the hills—
Paula knew her way around the bush,
and she'd grown up in those parts.
The mines were in a god-forsaken valley
in the high ranges miles from anywhere.
It was rough country, cut through
with creeks and gullies and thick
with stringy-bark scrub. The buildings—
sheds, an office, huge milling machines—
they'd been abandoned thirty years ago,
and they were standing silent in the heat.
The office was unlocked, and we went in.
Dust lay over everything, but otherwise

it was exactly as it used to be—
chair, desk, pens, blotting paper,
a set of balance scales weighing the dust,
bottles of dried purple and green ink,
rubber stamps. It gave me a strange feeling.
"Did they get much silver out of here?"
I asked. "Sure, way back," Paula said.
"Then it got scarce and uneconomical.
So they closed the mines. There are tunnels
you can get into, though they're boarded up.
I used to come here when I was a kid.
Go down deep enough and there's a river
that runs underground from the mountains
and forms a lake in a big limestone cave."
We looked into one of the tunnels.
A light rail track went down
into the darkness at a steep angle.
We climbed down about a hundred yards
till the rails disappeared in a pool
of water. I threw a stone, plop! My lighter
wasn't strong enough to show the other side.
Something about the colour of the water—
stained a dirty brown, dark and still—
reminded me of when Beth died,
the flooded river, and the muddy waves.
"And there's silver down there?" I asked.
I was thinking of my father's money.
"Yes, but not in rich veins," Paula said.
"It's kind of diluted, dispersed,
mixed up with lots of rock and stuff.
In the end it cost more to mine it
than they could get for it on the market."

I was thinking—in thirty years
mining technology must have improved.
They would have more efficient machinery
now. And this mine had been forgotten.
Paula was watching me. "Well," she said,
"Bob Kingston owns the mining rights,
if you're thinking of starting it up again."
Kingston? That was a blow. Like a dreamer,
I'd already begun planning how I'd
start the mine. A friend called Bellamy—
a hard drinker, I'd known him in Korea—
was now a mining engineer in Queensland.
And I had that money of my father's,
so I had cash to invest. But Kingston—
he wouldn't share anything with anybody.

'We drove back. I was silent, thinking.
My mind was whirling around and around.
"I'm not sure that showing you that mine
was such a good idea," Paula laughed.
"Let's have a swim," I said. I felt hot.
We swam awhile, then lay on the warm rocks.
Paula had a kind of animal grace;
she was strong, but lazy. And she could
sense what was in my mind; she was
one step ahead of me at every turn.
We made love there, for the first time.
I suppose it had to happen—we were
alone together in the heat of the bush:
the silence, not a soul for fifty miles.
Her eyes were a tiger-stone colour—
gold flecked with brown and green—

and she had a strange stare: it looked
right into you, deeper and deeper.

'On the drive back to town she drew away.
Perhaps she wanted to keep our intimacy
hidden in the bush, in the back country.
That was fine by me. I didn't
want anyone getting too close.
The months went by, and I sank into my work—
the darkroom was a perfect place to brood,
lit by the dim red safelight.
You could just make out the shapes
of the plate camera—it filled half the room—
and the developing tanks along the wall.
The sound of running water rippled
like an underground spring. I had
an old valve radio tuned in
to the ABC—symphony concerts,
the Country Hour, Blue Hills, and
late at night—it was always night in there—
the American Dance Band, and their smooth
unceasing optimism. Weeks went by
and I slowly came back to myself,
floating along on the rivers of sound.

'Paula called me one day. She was
getting her plane ready for the show.
"I'll give you a joy-ride," she said,
"for free." We met out at the airfield.
I didn't tell her I'd done some flying
in Korea. I think she wanted to test me.
It was a sports biplane, single motor,

and she threw that thing around the sky
like she was trying to break it in half.
Luckily I hadn't eaten any breakfast.
After a while she put the plane down
out by Devil's Lake, near the coast.
She'd brought a picnic basket, and some beer,
and we had a swim and then ate some lunch.
And then . . . one thing led to another.

'I felt strange about her, almost tender,
yet she was as tough as nails underneath
and there was something in her manner
I distrusted, something not right.
She was too much like me—hard, driven.
What did she have to be hard about?
"The weather got a bit rough up there,"
she said. "I hope you didn't mind the bumps."
"The weather was fine," I said. "No problem.
I'm looking forward to the trip home."
She laughed, and we dropped the subject.
"I talked to Kingston," she said. "He'll let you
open the mine. He's busy with the mill
and hasn't any time to spend on it, so
you'll have to do it alone: finance,
engineering, hiring men, administration.
He'll put in half the money, up to
eighty thousand; you find the rest.
He'll go fifty-fifty on the profits.
Okay?" I didn't know what to say.
How had she swung it? It didn't matter,
as long as I could get on with it
and make something useful of my life.

I told Bartlett—I often dropped by
in the evening, and usually stayed to dinner.
For a bachelor, he was a good cook.
That night I was so excited
by the plans buzzing around in my head
that I shovelled the food down. Bartlett listened,
but he didn't say anything. He looked awkward.
"It's not my business," he said in the end,
"but I'd stay clear of Bob Kingston
and Paula. People say—this is gossip,
I don't know why I'm repeating it—but
they reckon she's his daughter, illegitimate,
not that that matters these days,
and as far as I'm concerned it never did.
But to keep your daughter as your mistress,
that's too much for my stomach.
So I'd just keep a little distance
if I were you. But who wants advice?
Forget I said anything. Eat up."

'But my appetite was gone. Another blow.
Perhaps it was just malicious gossip—
small towns are poisonous like that—
but yes, there was something about Paula
that was wrong—I'd felt it from the start.
For a week or two I did nothing, then
I rang Bellamy, the engineer I knew
in Queensland, and talked about the mine.
He was game, and the idea intrigued him.
He came down and took a good look.

'"Some of the shafts are half flooded," he said,

"but a few pumps will soon fix that.
The ore looks to be medium grade,
but easy to get out. The market's firm.
You could break even in a few years.
From then on it should be steady profit."
And with those profits I could buy
shares in the name of a dummy company,
a few here, a few there, then
push Kingston out into the cold.
We were in action three months later.
We had a year of dry weather—drought,
was what the farmers called it. The pumps
had the tunnels dry within a month.
The mine had a lot more silver in it
deeper down, and with the new equipment
we were soon getting a good yield.
We broke even by the end of the year.

'Then Kingston sent a note demanding
cash for his share of the investment.
Nothing formal, just a note scribbled
in pencil on an old piece of paper.
His mill was going bad, he said, and
he needed the money to shore it up.
I went to the pub and asked to see him,
but he wasn't there. I found Paula
in a back room, changing into a frock
she often used to wear when she worked:
dark blue, with tiny pink flowers.
There was a plate of food on a side table—
a half-eaten chop, some vegetables—
and a cup of coffee, and a cigarette

smeared with lipstick stubbed in the saucer.
We'd hardly spoken in the last year.
He was away up the back country,
she said, scouting timber for the mill.
"Tell the bastard he'll get his money,"
I said, "in a year or two, if he wants it. But
I can't just tear half the investment
out of the mine. The bank would close us up.
Bellamy's broke. I've got nothing else.
Tell him he must understand that."

'"Oh, he understands," Paula said.
There was a sad, flat tone to her voice.
She had a hairpin between her teeth
while she fixed her hair in the mirror.
God, she was lovely. "I'm beginning to
regret I ever got you into this,"
she said. "Kingston has the legal right
to get his cash now, or take the mine."
Of course I knew how he operated—
unrealistic behaviour, inhuman demands.
There was no joy in it, just
a sick satisfaction in destruction.
There was an old cot in the corner.
I pushed Paula onto the bed, and kissed her.
We made love. It was quick and desperate,
more anger than love, and I felt cheated,
as though Kingston was in the room, watching
and laughing in that thin voice he had.
I drove back to the mine—the drought
had broken, it had rained for a week,
and all the pumps were working day and night.

Barry, the supervisor, said that Kingston
had turned up an hour before, soaking wet,
and had gone down Number Two tunnel
to poke around. He'd never been before,
and didn't know the safety regulations.
"Frankly, I'm worried," Barry said.
"He was yelling, and I couldn't stop him.
After all, he owns half the mine.
But Number Two's starting to fill with water,
and the river's rising up from below."
I didn't want to lose a major partner,
so I took a helmet and a piece of rope
and went in after him. A mile down
I came to a ford flooded with muddy water
washed down the underground river
from the hills and gullies up above.
Kingston was out there in the darkness
clinging to a crate. The rising water
had jammed it up against the tunnel roof.
"Hurry up," he said. "I'm bloody cold.
The water rose up and cut me off.
I can't swim. Hurry, throw a line."
He was too far for that, and the water
was deep. I tied one end of the rope
to a piece of track, and let myself
into the water, holding the other end.
It was freezing. "What were you doing?"
I had to yell above the sound of the river.
"You little shit," he said. "You're cheating!
There's no silver here. You and your mate
are milking me. I want my money back."
"There's nothing much here in Number Two,"

I said. "It's limestone. Number One's good;
and Number Three is full of bloody silver.
You got the assay reports. Can't you read?"
"And stay away from Paula," he yelled.
His voice was screeching, he was in a rage.
"I look after her, nobody else.
Understand?" I laughed. Here he was,
on the edge of the pit, and giving orders.
"Bring the rope here, for Christ's sake!"
But I couldn't; it wasn't long enough.
I'd have to let it go and swim to him,
and I wouldn't get back against the current,
not pulling the weight of both of us.
Kingston was being sucked into the dark.
He was finished, and I think he knew it.
My helmet lamp was fading, but the beam
picked out his eyes in the gloom.
His mouth was working, and he blew out
gasps of air. He was going under,
inch by inch. "Son," he said hoarsely,
"Help me. You bastard. Help me."
He was gasping between every word.
I couldn't let go of the rope,
we'd both die. "I can't," I said.
"Ah, fuck it!" he said, and he went under.
Where he'd been, there was just a bubble,
then nothing. My lamp was fading.

'I climbed up out of the tunnel,
in the dark, up to the windy evening.
The light was strange, dim and luminous,
heavy clouds were blowing out of the west.

I was so glad to breathe the air,
to feel the rain on my skin, I thought
I'll go on, I'll make money,
I'll climb up out of this shit.

'They never found Kingston's body.

'Paula left, she went to Singapore
with that plane of hers, she took up
with some French pilot and got lost
in the war they had there in Indo-China,
and no one heard from her again.
The mine? It petered out in the end,
just like it had years before.
I locked up the shop and walked away.
Oh, I got some money out of it,
but not much. I ended up in Sydney,
like I'd begun. Older. Alone again.

'What does it all mean? You tell me.
I've had it. I'm going to bed.'
Colin had stumbled off long ago;
I could hear him snoring faintly somewhere.
Jack stretched, and finished his bourbon,
and wandered inside. It was late;
I could hear a night-bird on the shore.

I went in and got a drink. Poor devil,
I thought; all that struggle for nothing.
Then I remembered a pair of drug runners
I'd met in Thailand—middle-aged men
but full of energy, heavy drinkers,

flying a light plane up to Burma,
taking risks to make a lot of money
to take home to their families in Marseilles—
one had proudly shown me a photo
of his blonde young wife and baby son—
both now in jail in Bangkok,
for life. Maybe twenty young lives
had been saved; but when I turned them in,
had I really done the right thing?
And Kathy, struggling too, and in the end
losing—what had she lost—her promise?
But she still had a kind of faith,
going on with her life and her work.

RAIN

PART THREE

When I came out Kathy was standing
by the railing, looking up at the sky.
You could see a few stars, here and there,
glinting through the patchwork cloud.
I lit cigarettes for us both
and we leant on the rail, side by side,
just as we had on the ferry on the way up.
She was wearing slacks and a silk blouse,
grey, with tiny yellow polka-dots,
and a perfume, something soft and delicate.
After a while Kathy broke the silence.

'Do you ever think,' she asked, 'that there's
some pattern in things, a kind of balance?
The Indians have this idea of karma,
where everything is added up, and you pay
for bad things, and do well if you're good.
But that's just childish, isn't it?
I don't know what the pattern is.
Maybe there isn't one, just the law.
When Trent was crippled in the crash
I felt responsible—well, I was,
in a way, but the drugs, the setup,
that other couple, the whole evening—
it was a rotten game that went wrong.
In America everything has a ticket.
Trent fumbled the deal, and paid the price.

Do you think that's why it happened?'
I shrugged my shoulders. She went on—
'After that little episode
I tried to make things work with Colin.
You can imagine I felt shaken up,
but Colin was at the bottom of the pit.
The big show he'd been working on,
it fell through when Trent was convicted
and went to jail. Trent's name was poison.
No New York gallery would touch him.
Anyone who'd been connected with him
was the same. They all took drugs,
it wasn't that: it was getting caught.
Colin's paintings were good—well,
looking back on them, they weren't
earth-shattering, but they were as good
as most of the rubbish being shown then.
But it was no use, no one wanted it,
they wanted the new thing then,
the post-abstract thing from Germany,
that wet Romantic landscape stuff,
West Coast Realism, other fashions,
and Colin had lost the strength to keep
making it new every goddamn day,
so he never made it in the States,
and New York was just a nightmare,
a bad dream that cost us a fortune.

'And then the accident happened.
Colin was minding the kid, but
he was drunk again, I should have known
it wasn't safe to leave him with Colin

but I had to get out of the place
once in a while. I'd go to a bar
on Tenth Street and drink a bit.
Timmy ran out onto the street—
he was chasing a kitten, someone said—
and a truck full of fur coats hit him.
Poor little kid—he lived for a week,
a week doesn't seem long, does it?
But it was a lifetime for Timmy.
After that, nothing mattered. Nothing.
Not Colin, not his bullshit painting,
not that rotten business with Trent.
My whole life looked like a bad road
that led up to this week of torment,
and yet it meant nothing. Maybe—'
she seemed to find it hard to speak—
'maybe if I'd gone mad; or into a convent,
to devote myself to God; maybe if I'd
written it all down like a novel,
and learnt how to become a great soul
with significant things to say about pain,
how the most innocent are made to suffer—'
Kathy was sobbing at last, the tears
running down her cheeks onto her blouse—
'but no, my life wound up in a heap
at the side of that wretched little cot
in a New York slum hospital, and
it all ended in a tiny, painful death,
and I can't find any meaning in it.'

I let her cry. What could I say? People
don't live and die for a purpose,

like a character introduced in a movie
and done away with in the final scene
so the plot will turn out right.
Life was a mystery, with no explanation.
How can you talk about that? The water
and the clouds and the starlight had been
just like that for a million years,
and a hundred million lives had come and gone.
If you dwelt on those things, you'd go mad.
I looked down into the water. I could see
sheets of phosphorescent plankton rippling
deep down under the boat, shimmering
electric veils, pale green and blue.
Kathy leant against me. 'It's getting cold,'
she said, and I put my arm around her shoulder.

When we went inside we found
Colin fast asleep on the bed
I'd meant to use, in the living room.
Jack was snoring on the other bunk.
'We'll just have to share the double bed,'
Kathy said. 'Is that all right with you?'
We took the bourbon into the bedroom
and undressed with our backs to each other
and slipped in between the sheets. Her leg
lay against mine. A street lamp
from the footpath on the shore outside
made mottled pools of light dip and
ripple on the ceiling above our bed.
I let my hand rest on her arm, just
touching. 'Tell me about Colin,' I said.
'He wasn't into morphine when you left.'

'Oh, you don't want to hear all that.
I've been boring you. You must be tired.'
'Go on,' I said. 'I'm not, if you're not.'
Her skin was cool. I felt my fingers must be
burning her arm. Why didn't she pull away?

'Colin got drunk at a party,' she said.
'He did a lot of that, after Timmy died.
He was drunk, and he got into an argument
about masculinity and action painting
at a party this rich painter was holding
on a boat out on the East River.
Klassky was his name, and he'd made it.
Oh, there were rich painters, and then
there were painters who weren't rich at all.
The argument got violent, and Klassky
pushed Colin—he didn't mean to hurt him,
but Colin tripped sideways down a ladder
and his head slammed against a winch fitting
and he injured the side of his face. He got up
and knocked Klassky down with one hit.
Colin thought he'd killed him at first,
but he hadn't—he'd knocked him out,
and when Klassky fell he struck his head
on the railing, and the skull was fractured.
It caused a blood clot on the brain.
It took a few days for all this
to come out, and the waiting was awful.
They kept them both in hospital for weeks,
but very different ones, believe me.
When Colin's face had been patched up
he went to apologise to Klassky.

He was anxious about it, and jumpy.
They'd given him morphine in the hospital
because of the fractures in his facial bones.
By the time he got out he was addicted,
shaky, and going through withdrawal.
Klassky had a reputation for violence.
He'd broken a woman's nose once at a party
after an argument about Picasso, and
he'd knocked out an art critic's teeth.
But Colin, when he went to visit, found
a changed man. The doctors had him on sedatives,
and he kept the curtains drawn against the light.
He was in a wheelchair, and he dozed off
from time to time. Friends would read to him.
He liked religious books, the lives of the saints.
I guess he'd developed a fixation of some kind—
his mother was religious, from the old country,
always going to church and praying a lot.
When Colin said he was sorry, Klassky
burst into tears, and hugged him. Colin
came back to sit with him again,
and offered to read to him, and in the end
he became a regular visitor, and a friend.
Colin was painting less, drawing a little,
maybe a watercolour or two of an evening,
tiny sketches in ink and sepia wash.
He started taking Klassky out for walks
every day, and always at dawn—
there was less traffic, it was easier
with the wheelchair, and Colin said
the peaceful atmosphere seemed to help—
he'd calm down and focus on his drawings

through the rest of the day. The Jungle
showed a different side then, I guess.
I'd go with them some mornings,
when I'd finished in the darkroom.
Klassky didn't seem to mind being
in a wheelchair. He'd made a lot of money,
and invested it well, so he had an income.
On Sundays he liked to go to church,
the Serbian Orthodox on Twenty-Fifth,
and he'd sit there for maybe an hour
inhaling the incense, murmuring to himself.
In the end he became a convert
to the Catholic Church. He sends us postcards,
scenes of martyrdom, that kind of thing.
We heard he went to Rome last year,
and had a private audience with Guess Who.

'Well, the money ran out, eventually,
and that was the end of our American Dream.
We came back to Sydney, we separated.
We're still friends, we went through
too much together not to be.
Colin got a job at the hospital,
helping kids with colour therapy.
And of course he brought back his problem.
And I have my photography. As you know
there's not much money in that.
Oh, I could do corporate accounts,
but can you imagine me shooting
some advertising fuckwit in a Porsche?
And keeping a straight face? Not likely.
I do what I have to do, and I survive.'

Kathy finished her drink, and lay back.
'I think that's enough bourbon,' she said.
'And you?' I could feel she was looking at me
in the dark. 'What were you up to,
while I was going crazy in New York?'

I thought about California,
my brother dead on his motor bike,
studying at night for my degree, Thailand,
a marriage that hadn't turned out well.
'I can't start all that,' I said.
'You don't want to hear about buildings,
and the personal stuff is too complicated.
Let's go to sleep.' I didn't want to sleep,
I wanted to make love to Kathy, but
it all seemed confused and impossible.

'You can tell me some other time,' she said.
She kissed me on the lips, and her voice
came murmuring into my mouth. 'Oh Sandra,'
she said, and she was moving in my arms.